# Installing & Renewing Lawns

# Installing & Renewing Lawns

**WRITER**
Anne M. Zeman

**PHOTOGRAPHERS**
Alan Copeland and Barry Shapiro

**ILLUSTRATOR**
James Balkovek

Lawn & Garden

Product Manager: CYNTHIA FOLLAND, NK LAWN & GARDEN CO.

Acquisition, Development and Production Services: BMR, Corte Madera, CA

Acquisition: JACK JENNINGS, BOB DOLEZAL
Series Concept: BOB DOLEZAL
Project Director: JANE RYAN
Developmental Editor: KATE KELLY
Horticulturist: BARBARA STREMPLE
Photographic Director: ALAN COPELAND
Art Director (cover): KARRYLL NASON
Art Director (interior): BRAD GREENE
Cover Design: KAREN EMERSON
Cover Stylist: JOANN MASAOKA VAN ATTA
Cover Photo: BARRY SHAPIRO
Interior Art: JAMES BALKOVEK
North American Map: RON HILDEBRAND
Site Scout: PEGGY HENRY, PAT TALBERT
Photo Assistant: LISA PISCHEL
Copy Editor: JANET VOLKMAN
Proofreader: LYNN FERAR
Typography and Page Layout: BARBARA GELFAND
Index: SYLVIA COATES
Color Separations: PREPRESS ASSEMBLY INCORPORATED
Printing and Binding: PENDELL PRINTING INC.
Production Management: THOMAS E. DORSANEO, JANE RYAN

INSTALLING AND RENEWING LAWNS Copyright © 1992 by NK Lawn & Garden Co. All rights reserved. Printed in the United States of America. No part of this book may be used or reproduced in any manner whatsoever without written permission except in the case of brief quotations embodied in critical articles and reviews. For information address BMR, 21 Tamal Vista Blvd., Corte Madera, CA 94925.

First Edition

Library of Congress Cataloging-in-Publication Data:
Zeman, Anne M.
   Installing and renewing lawns / writer, Anne Zeman ; photographers Alan Copeland and Barry Shapiro ; illustrator, James Balkovek.
    p. cm. -- (NK Lawn & Garden step-by-step visual guide)
  Includes index.
  ISBN : 1-880281-10-4
  1. Lawns. I. Title. II. Series.
SB433.Z46 1993
635.9'647--dc20                      92-20215
                                        CIP

Special thanks to Mike Strunk, Park Avenue Turf, Sebastopol, CA, for grasses featured on pgs. 68–75.

Also special thanks to: Emeigh and David Poindexter, Anne Wagner, Maria Poindexter, Polly Elliott, Katherine Kirk, and Janet Pischel.

Additional photo credits: Saxon Holt, pgs. 30-31, 42-43, 56 (crabgrass).

**Notice:** The information contained in this book is true and complete to the best of our knowledge. All recommendations are made without any guarantees on the part of the authors, NK Lawn & Garden Co., or BMR. Because the means, materials and procedures followed by homeowners are beyond our control, the author and publisher disclaim all liability in connection with the use of this information.

92  93  94  95  96   10  9  8  7  6  5  4  3  2  1

# TABLE OF CONTENTS

Planting New Lawns: Overview ............................. 6–7
New or Renew ................................................... 8–9
Professional Help ............................................. 10–11
Minor Lawn Repair ........................................... 12–13
Major Lawn Renovation I ................................... 14–15
Major Lawn Renovation II .................................. 16–17
Removing Old Lawns ......................................... 18–19
Preparing The Site ............................................ 20–21
Grading and Drainage ....................................... 22–23
Analyzing Your Soil .......................................... 24–25
Preparing the Soil ............................................. 26–27
Amending Soils ................................................ 28–29
Lime and Sulfur ................................................ 30–31
Installing In-Ground Irrigation I .......................... 32–33
Installing In-Ground Irrigation II ......................... 34–35
Analyzing Your Grass Needs ............................... 36–37
Seed, Sod, Plug, or Sprig ................................... 38–39
Choosing Grass Mixtures ................................... 40–41
Choosing Grass Seed ........................................ 42–43
Planting Lawns From Seed ................................. 44–45
Planting Lawns From Sod .................................. 46–47
Planting Lawns From Sprigs and Plugs ................ 48–49
Watering ......................................................... 50–51
Mowing ........................................................... 52–53
Fertilizing ........................................................ 54–55
Annual Maintenance ......................................... 56–57
Long-Term Maintenance .................................... 58–59
Alternatives to Turfgrass ................................... 60–61
Planting Broadleaf Groundcovers ....................... 62–63
Climate Map of Turfgrasses ............................... 64–65
Regional Differences ......................................... 66–67
Cool-Season Grass I .......................................... 68–69
Cool-Season Grass II ......................................... 70–71
Warm-Season Grass I ........................................ 72–73
Warm-Season Grass II ....................................... 74–75
Tools and Equipment ........................................ 76–77
Index .............................................................. 78–79

# Planting New Lawns: Overview

## Steps to Success

Fresh paint, glimmering windows and a luxuriant lawn are the hallmarks of a well-tended home. But like house paint and windows, lawns grow a bit shabby over time and require care and attention to maintain a fresh, tidy appearance.

Growing and maintaining a beautiful lawn requires more effort than simply throwing down a few seeds and hoping for the best. But a rich carpet of grass can be yours if you follow a few simple steps. First you need to assess your lawn to determine its general condition, trouble spots, etc. Established lawns will probably need renovation of some kind, either minor or major. Sooner or later all lawns will need dethatching or aeration.

If you have an extremely poor lawn, where 50–60 percent is dead, you should probably remove the old grass and weeds and start all over. Most lawns, however, need only renovation—from dethatching and aerating to spot seeding—to restore beauty.

To install a new lawn, whether from seed, sod, sprigs or plugs, be sure to prepare the soil. In fact, soil preparation is the most important thing you'll do. Test your soil to determine its quality and composition and add any necessary amendments. Apply plenty of organic matter and fertilize before planting. Choose from a wide range of lawn grasses, depending on your lifestyle and individual needs, and determine how you want to plant your lawn—by sowing seed, laying sod or planting plugs or sprigs.

**First** Assess your lawn to determine what needs to be done to improve it. Minor renovations may be all that is needed. However, aeration for soil compaction, dethatching for thatch buildup and overseeding may be necessary on older or neglected lawns (see pgs. 12–17).

**Or** If your lawn is more than 50–60 percent dead, remove the old lawn and prepare the site. Renovation will improve the majority of lawns, and only when the lawn is dead, bare or the soil severely compacted will removal be necessary (see pgs. 18–19).

**Then** Test soil for nutrients, adjust pH. The best pH for most lawns is 6.0–6.5. Depending on where you live and the condition of your soil, it may be necessary to add lime or sulfur to adjust pH to the proper levels (see pgs. 24–25).

**Fourth** Choose a turfgrass that is best suited for your area. Understand your climate and zone. Then choose a lawn seed that performs well under local conditions and know the extent of its maintenance needs (see pgs. 68–75).

**Third** Improving your soil by adding amendments will significantly reduce lawn problems. Preparation of soil cannot be overemphasized. Determine your soil type and add organic matter and other amendments, if necessary. Fertilize at least once a year (see pgs. 26–31).

**Last** Plant a new lawn by seeding, sodding or plugging. Seeding is the most popular and least expensive; sodding yields instant results, but costs more. In warm-season areas, you have the option of using plugs or sprigs (see pgs. 36–49).

# NEW OR RENEW

## GETTING STARTED

If you have a brand new home, you have the opportunity to start a beautiful new lawn and to do it right. If you have an older home, even a year or two old, you have inherited a lawn, usually in need of some kind of repair.

A lush, green lawn for sitting, walking and playing upon can be yours if you understand a few simple facts about lawn grass: how it grows, what it needs in order to thrive and the importance of choosing the right grass for your climate. Maintenance is not difficult and not nearly as complicated as many make it out to be. In fact, many people perform maintenance tasks more often than really necessary.

Before you start on a new lawn or renovate an old one, you should consider the use of your lawn. You may need a fenced play area for children. If you enjoy entertaining, you may want to eliminate some of the lawn for a terrace or deck. If you have little leisure time, you may want to consider choosing a groundcover alternative to turfgrass. Analyzing your needs can save you time and money in the long run.

Evaluation of your property is critical in understanding what needs to be renovated. Different areas of your lawn will require different methods. Whether renovating or starting an entirely new lawn, this book will guide you in an easy, step-by-step format.

Bare spots are the most common lawn problems and are the result of poor drainage, disease, insect damage or traffic.

Disease and insect damage are usually characterized by discoloring, spots or rings.

Weeds are plants that grow where they aren't wanted. Weeds may be broadleaf or grass types.

Areas of small dead or dying patches are often caused by grubs. Spilled gasoline, oil or a dog can also be the cause.

Thin growth or no grass growth is often the result of shade; lawn grasses do not grow well in deep shade. Thin growth in the sun may also be due to thatch, compaction or poor soil.

# EVALUATING YOUR LAWN

The best way to begin an evaluation of your lawn is to take a walk around your property. What is the overall effect of your lawn? Is it green and thick, or is it thin or sparse? Does it have bare places or clumps of grass? Look for trouble spots—brown areas, dead patches or discolored grass. Are weeds choking your lawn? Is it an old lawn that has been neglected and become shabby? Make a checklist of the problems to determine if you need to renew your lawn or start a new one.

Many patchy, dying lawns are suffering from soil compaction or thatch buildup. Soil compaction is characterized by hard, solid ground, usually with yellowing or pale green grass that has begun to die. This condition deprives the lawn grass of the oxygen, water and fertilizer it needs to grow. Thatch also deprives the grass of nutrients by blocking the penetration of water and fertilizer. Thus, renovation by dethatching or aerating can greatly improve your lawn.

If the existing lawn still has a reasonable proportion of good grasses, a renovation program of fertilization, watering and weed control can do a lot to restore the beauty of your lawn. If the better grasses have been crowded out by weeds and inferior grasses and have become dominant, your lawn is a good candidate for starting over. To find out what type of grass you have, take a sample to your nursery.

It is important to determine not only if your lawn has problems, but also the extent of any deterioration. If thatch, soil compaction, weeds or inferior grasses are widespread, it might well be simpler to start a new lawn than to do battle with these pervasive problems. As a rule, most lawns can be revived through renovation and overseeding; however, if 50–60 percent is dead, bare or covered with weeds, it is best to start over.

# Professional Help

## Tips on Hiring a Professional

When searching for a lawn professional, keep these things in mind:

**Meet with the professional**  Have the professional come to your property and walk it with you. Ask questions and get specific opinions and recommendations for your lawn.

**Ask for a personalized program**  Some companies offer the exact same service to everyone. Find out specifically what this is and ask if they will tailor the program to your needs.

**Chemicals or not?**  Some lawn services, particularly maintenance services, offer chemical-free treatments. Be sure to ask.

**Inquire about equipment**  Find out what kind of equipment is used for big jobs. If the professional is charging you by the hour, he or she will save time and money with faster and more sophisticated equipment.

**Get three estimates**  Understand how you will be charged—by the job performed or by the hour and if there are minimum requirements.

**Ask for a contract**  Put terms in writing so there is no misunderstanding on either side.

**Ask for credentials**  Ask how long the professional has been in business and verify his or her level of training and experience. If an herbicide or pesticide treatment is used, ask if the professional is licensed to apply them. A homeowner can apply some chemicals, but others must be applied by a licensed contractor.

This lawn can be renovated by dethatching, aerating, fertilizing and reseeding.

## Do It Yourself or Hire a Professional?

If you've decided that major renovation is needed, or if you need to install a new lawn, you may want to consider using a professional. Time and expense are the major factors. If you have the time and the inclination to do it yourself, none of these chores is difficult. But they can be time-consuming. Aeration or dethatching can usually be done in a weekend, but installing a new lawn will probably take several days, depending on the size of your property.

First, decide what you want to have done. If you are unsure, call a professional lawn-care specialist or an agricultural extension agent for an evaluation. There's no obligation for a consultation and estimate. It's always recommended to get more than one opinion and estimate.

There are a number of lawn-care specialists listed in the phone book. Many specialize in seeding and routine maintenance only. Inquire whether they have the equipment to aerate and dethatch. Landscape contractors will also be listed in the phone book as performing similar tasks. If you choose a landscape contractor and wish to have herbicide and pesticide treatments, make sure they are licensed for this work.

Professional help offers many rewards—and a few drawbacks. Professionals usually have far greater knowledge and experience for identifying and solving problems; they have larger and more sophisticated equipment and crews, making the job go easier and faster, and most offer guarantees. The biggest asset may be the time they save you from doing the work. The drawbacks are expense—most require a multivisit contract or a minimum fee.

# Minor Lawn Repair

**Bare Spots** Bare spots usually no larger than 8–12 in. across. Caused by drainage, disease, insects, traffic.
**Solution** Reseed spots. Remove dead grass and loosen soil to 4–5 in. Add amendments and level. Spread seed, lightly rake into soil, firm, water. Rope off if necessary.

**Weed Spots** Areas where weeds have choked out preferred grass—usually in sections but spreading.
**Solution** For small areas, pull by hand. In large areas, use a rotary tiller. Ask nursery about chemical options. If lawn is overrun, eliminate lawn and start over.

**Brown Patches** Dead or dying grass in patches or rings. Caused by fungus. Bentgrass, St. Augustine grass and tall fescue are most often attacked.
**Solution** You can discourage—but not cure—brown patch disease. Fertilize in proper amounts. Lower soil pH with an acidic fertilizer. Provide good drainage. Overseed with less susceptible grass varieties. Apply fungicide with nursery guidance.

**Damaged Areas** Bare, brown or yellowing areas. Causes: fertilizer burn, insects, spilled gasoline or herbicide, dog urine.
**Solution** Patch with seed or sod. See "Bare Spots" above. For fertilizer burns, soak with water; avoid fertilizing in hot months.

Repair bare spots by loosening and amending the soil, seeding, lightly raking, firming the soil and watering.

## Restoring Your Lawn

Sooner or later every lawn needs some kind of repair. Most repairs are minor and require only a little effort.

Bare spots show up even on the best of lawns. Foot traffic or soil compaction are usually the cause. Brown spots or patches also appear and can be caused by gasoline spills or the neighbor's dog. Many times, however, they can be caused by a fungus or disease.

Examine the soil and lawn grass at close range to determine the causes of insect damage and disease. Small dead patches may be caused by grubs. Close inspection of grass blades reveal telltale signs of other insect damage. Insects can be active year round, although they are usually inactive during winter months in cooler regions. Good lawn maintenance practices will keep pests to a minimum.

Diseases often cause yellow discoloring or spots on the leaves. These are all fairly easy to correct. A more serious problem is brown patch caused by a fungus promoted by hot and humid weather. Oftentimes, this area will have to be replaced and reseeded. A common problem of bluegrass lawns is fusarium blight, a soil-borne fungus that attacks lawns stressed by too much water and nitrogen. Yellow grass can be caused by a lack of nitrogen and corrected with fertilizer.

If you live in the northern United States or Canada, pavement salt may damage patches of lawn along sidewalks, driveways and curbsides. Choose a salt-tolerant grass such as 'Fults' *Puccinellia distans*. Instead of salting your walks and driveway, try using sand.

# Major Lawn Renovation I

## Dethatching and Aerification

If your lawn looks thin, yet more than 50 percent is covered with good grass, it is time to renovate. Two common problems that contribute to poor lawn are *thatch buildup* and *soil compaction*.

Thatch is the tan layer of grass and leaf debris that builds up above the soil surface. When the thatch layer is over one-half inch thick, it mats together, preventing water and fertilizer from reaching the soil. Thatch causes the grass to grow above the soil surface where the roots are subject to drying out, freezing, and injury from disease, pests and foot traffic.

Remove thatch with a dethatching machine. It has vertical blades that cut through the thatch, bringing it to the surface. Finish by raking the thatch off the lawn. Dethatch in the fall for cool-season grasses, and in the spring or early summer for warm-season grasses. To prevent thatch from building up again, mow more often or use a mulching mower.

Compacted soil also prevents air, water, and nutrients from getting to the roots. Use an aerator to loosen compacted soil. Avoid aerators that do not lift out cores of soil; they contribute to soil compaction. The holes left by the soil cores enable air, water and nutrients to reach the roots. Aerify when the grass is growing, in the spring or fall, when temperatures are cool and the ground is moist.

After dethatching and aerifying, overseed with a quality lawn seed mixture to prevent weeds from becoming established. To keep your lawn healthy, plan on dethatching and aerifying every three to five years.

## Dethatching

**First** Cut a 3 in. square by 3 in. deep section of grass. Examine the cross section. If there is more than 1/2 in. of spongy, thick thatch, dethatching is necessary.

**Next** Rent a dethatcher and set the blades to penetrate the thatch layer and the top 1/4 in. of soil. Run over the lawn twice at 45° angles.

**Last** Rake thoroughly. Overseed with a quality lawn seed mixture.

## Aerification

**First** Compacted soil kills grass by blocking nutrients, air and water to grass roots.

**Next** Rent an aerification machine to penetrate 2-3 in. and remove cores of soil. Make two passes over your lawn at 45° angles.

**Last** Rake cores or leave on lawn to dry and crumble. Overseed with a quality lawn seed mixture.

# Major Lawn Renovation II

## Renovations and Overseeding

Overseeding—planting grass seed into an existing lawn without removing or tearing up the turf or the soil—requires less labor, less time and provides more cover to protect against wind or water erosion than digging out and reseeding lawn patches. The benefits of overseeding include improved density of the lawn grass, filled in bare spots, improved grass varieties and enhanced lawn color.

Before you overseed, determine why your turf has deteriorated or died out. Soil compaction, thatch, improper drainage, shade or lack of fertilizer or water may be the problems. If any of these conditions is not corrected, your newly overseeded lawn may deteriorate as well. If you are unsure, contact your local county extension office or lawn professionals for an evaluation.

If your home is ten years old or more, you may have a type of lawn grass that is more prone to disease and insects. Overseed with newer turfgrass varieties that have been bred to withstand disease, insects, drought, shade and heavy traffic. Your payback will be in the reduction of pesticides, fertilizer and water you'll need.

Winter overseeding—sowing quick-growing grass seed over an existing dormant lawn—is another alternative in milder climates. It is a common practice in southern states to sow annual or perennial ryegrass over dormant warm-season grasses in early winter to have a luxuriant lawn all winter.

# OVERSEEDING TIPS

## Overseed

- If your home lawn is 10 years old or more and has been generally neglected.
- If current grass is an older variety that is not disease, insect or drought resistant. Choose a grass variety that has been developed for these specific purposes.
- When lawns have become thin and sparse due to disease or shade.
- When drought has destroyed a substantial portion of the lawn.
- When the old grass has deteriorated or has begun to die out.
- If you have a number of bare areas or just need a general sprucing up.

## When Is the Best Time to Overseed?

- **Late summer/early fall** This is the best time to overseed lawns for cool-season grasses. Weed competition is greatly reduced, giving newly planted seedlings a better chance to develop. This time of year also provides for favorable soil and atmospheric temperatures for seed germination.
- **Spring** If you cannot overseed in early fall, spring is the next best time; however, there is a greater chance for weather problems, such as heavy rains. If overseeding at this time, delay any application of herbicides—this will interfere with seedling establishment.

To overseed a lawn, mow the grass and aerate thoroughly, using a core-type aerator. Fertilize with a good starter fertilizer, applying at the recommended rate. Reseed using the recommended rate for overseeding. Make two passes at 45° angles.

# REMOVING OLD LAWNS

## REMOVAL METHODS

Even if your lawn is 50-60 percent dead or bare, you can probably revive it through proper renovation. Should your lawn have less than 40 percent healthy turf, or if grass is patchy and the soil hard packed and lacking water-holding humus, complete renovation and replanting may be your best alternative. This involves removing or killing the existing turf and weeds, and reseeding or sodding the entire lawn.

Removing grass is best done with a sod cutter, a machine readily available at rental stores. It is relatively easy to use, making quick work of removing the grass. Be sure the setting is on low—you only want to take off the vegetative layer, not remove topsoil. Sod can also be taken out by hand with a spade or with a tiller. Afterward you will need to prepare the soil before planting. You can use the tiller for both—getting rid of the sod on the first pass and preparing the soil in successive passes.

You can eliminate grass and vegetation on small areas with black plastic. Purchase large rolls, lay it on the damaged areas, secure it and wait a few weeks. The plastic cover kills the plants beneath it. The only drawback is the eyesore of a plastic-littered yard.

A lawn can also be removed with chemicals by applying a glyphosate-type product to the entire area. Use caution when using any type of chemical and use only as directed.

Sod cutters are available at rental stores.

**Black Plastic** Purchase rolls in minimum lengths of 15 ft. Cover all vegetative areas. Secure with wooden pegs or sod pins. All growth will be smothered in approximately 3–4 weeks, sooner if weather is hot.

**Rotary Tiller** To remove vegetation, set the depth at 2–3 in. and make a first pass. Rake and discard all grass clumps and weeds. Make a second pass, if needed; otherwise, to begin soil preparation, set the depth at 6–8 in., turn the soil and add amendments.

# PREPARING THE SITE

Preparing a site for a new lawn installation may require several steps, from clearing the area of construction debris to rough grading. Plan where you want foundation plantings and groundcovers and install lawn edgings to restrict their growth to intended areas.

## Preparation

**First** Remove all debris including construction materials, large stones, roots and any weeds.

**Third** If necessary, use a steel landscape rake to rough grade, making a gradual slope away from the house (see pgs. 22–23).

**Next** Make sure all subsurface drains are free of debris.

**Then** Carefully rake lawn area.

**Fourth** Check for puddling or areas where water is standing and not draining properly.

**Last** Fill in puddles and low spots, then level in preparation for planting.

### Installing Lawn Edgings

**First** Purchase steel, aluminum or polyethylene strip edging. Dig a trench as deep as the width of the edging between the lawn and planting area.

**Then** Place the edging just above the root zone of the grass, level with the top of the soil.

**Next** Stake edging in place, securing it at both ends.

**Last** Backfill and level, leaving soil a maximum 1 in. lower on the planting side.

# NEW HOME SITES

If you have just purchased a new home, you have a number of options concerning your lawn. If you've purchased your house before building is completed, you can work with the developer or builder to choose an appropriate lawn and landscape scheme—including the choice of grass seed or sod. Often landscaping is included in the price of the house and you can also choose other features, such as shrubs and groundcovers.

Many new lawns are started on soil that has been removed from foundation excavations. This subsoil is usually dense and hard with no organic matter. It is best to replace it with new topsoil. Have the developer save the topsoil from the entire lot before building begins. This can be used for the new lawn. The developer usually does the grading of the lot; however, new homes today often have level lots. You'll need a slight grade for runoff (see pgs. 22–23).

Soil preparation is the first step in installing a new lawn. A bare construction site offers a full range of options for lawn installation—and a perfect opportunity to install it right. Start with the soil to ensure success. It will take a bit longer than just sowing grass seed on the existing area but will be far less expensive in the long run with lasting results.

# GRADING AND DRAINAGE

**Terraced Slope** The slope of supporting banks should conform to that of the area used to ascend them. The maximum slope for this is 1 ft. rise for 2 ft. distance.

**Testing Drainage** Dig a hole 1 ft. across and 2 ft. deep. Fill it with water and begin timing for drainage. If the water takes more than 15 minutes to drain, soil is too dense and you may need to put in drainage tiles.

## Lawns and Grading

The surface or slope of a ground surface is called the *grade*. Grading is the shaping of the ground surface to produce useful contours.

Grading is usually done by experts, but the homeowner can do rough grading. All grading should be done as early as possible. If your entire property needs grading, it is best to remove the topsoil and stockpile it out of the way. If paths and driveways are to be laid out, outline and stake these areas. Loosen the subsoil and contour as needed by filling to raise it or by removing subsoil to lower it, using a carpenter's or mason's level as an aid in establishing grades. Slope the grade as gradually as possible away from the house, creating a pitch of one foot for every 20–25 feet. However, a rise of one foot in four is about the limit for a successful lawn. Anything more than this will need to be terraced. A lawn requires at least six to eight inches of topsoil above the subgrade. Make sure when you return the topsoil that you have an adequate amount.

When raising or lowering the grade a foot or more, take precautions to protect trees. Putting 12 inches of soil around a tree could seriously injure it by reducing the amount of air and water reaching the roots. Build a well of three to four feet around the tree to protect it. If lowering the contour around a tree, take care not to cut the roots of the tree by leaving a mounded area around it.

Adequate drainage is required for all lawns. Your property must have sufficient slope to carry off surface water so that it will not collect and cause damage to the grass or plants. A good lawn can never grow on waterlogged soil.

Level off the foundation area for plantings and begin grading from here. A proper job of grading should eliminate all steep areas of over 25° slope. For a new home, remove valuable topsoil from the area staked for the driveway to reuse on the lawn. A pitch of 1 ft. for every 20–25 ft. is adequate for drainage. Grade and excavate all areas that puddle or are intended for run-off.

# ANALYZING YOUR SOIL

## SOIL TESTING

Whether you are installing a new lawn or renovating an old one, the first thing you should do is have your soil tested. Soil tests yield valuable information on soil structure and nutrients (nitrogen (N), phosphorus (P), potassium (K), and micronutrients). You will then know which amendments are needed for best lawn growth.

To test the soil, take soil samples from three to five different areas on your property. This way the test will give a general reading for the site. Use a hollow soil sampling tube to extract your soil. Or dig a hole several inches down and take samples from the sides of the hole. Make sure you get more than just the topsoil.

Whether you perform your own soil tests or send a sample to a nearby Agricultural Extension Service, nursery or college soil lab, you will need to interpret the results. Among the readings of your soil test, you'll find the critical measure of your soil's acidity or alkalinity—known as the pH reading. This number represents a scale from 0–14, with 7 being the center and neutral, lower numbers denoting acidity and higher numbers alkalinity. Soils in the East, Midwest and Northwest tend to be acid, while soils in the West tend to be alkaline. A soil pH between 6.0 and 6.5 is optimal for most lawn grass growth, although some grasses thrive in acid soil with a pH as low as 4.0, and many grasses thrive in alkaline soil with a pH up to 8.5. Adjusting the acidity and alkalinity of the soil allows the fertilizer to become more soluble, thus enabling the grass to use vital nutrients.

**Taking a Soil Sample** Use a hollow soil sampler tube to extract a deep sample of your soil to send to your Agricultural Extension Service. Your local service can be found by checking county or state listings in your phone book.

**Soil Test Kits** Many kinds of at-home soil testing equipment are available in a wide range of prices. Discuss best selections with your garden center specialist. As a rule, none are as reliable as the extension service.

**Sandy Soil**  Sandy soil features large, individual mineral particles, a lot of air space and crumbles easily when squeezed. Often called "light" soil, it permits roots to penetrate readily, but allows water and nutrients to drain away quickly. Compost and peat moss are both good amendments to add to sandy soil.

**Clay Soil**  Clay soil is made up of very tiny inorganic particles. It is often called "heavy" soil because the particles pack together densely holding water and impairing drainage. Wet clay is sticky and holds firm. Dry clay is hard. Compost is an excellent conditioner to add to clay soil.

**Silt Soil**  Silt has moderate-sized mineral particles that are larger than clay and smaller than sand. Dry silt, when squeezed, breaks up and is lumpy. It retains water well but lacks important air space between particles. Add organic matter to improve soil with too much silt.

**Loam Soil**  Often called the ideal soil, loam contains nearly equal parts of clay, silt, sand and organic matter. It retains moisture, air and nutrients yet drains easily. It is also referred to as "loose" or "friable" soil.

# Preparing the Soil

## How to Prepare the Soil

The only sure way to get the beautiful lawn you've always wanted is by preparing the soil carefully before planting. Unlike flower or vegetable gardens where soil can be rebuilt every year, grass roots remain in the same soil year after year. Nutrients can be added to an established lawn, but the basic soil structure from which the grass grows is not easily or inexpensively altered.

Grass does not grow well either in impenetrable, hard-packed clay or in loose, sandy soil. Both soils lack humus or organic matter. Clay soils are poorly aerated, dense and hold considerable water, making drainage difficult. Sandy soils have too much air and too low a capacity to hold water. Both clay and sandy soils, then, prevent essential nutrients from reaching the root systems and so provide poor conditions for growing vigorous lawn grasses.

Lawn soil needs to be loose and friable, or slightly crumbly. Till the soil, that is, prepare the soil for the cultivation of grass, using a spade, digging fork, plow or rotary tiller to turn the soil over, making it easier to add and mix manures and other amendments.

Rotary tillers are the easiest way for most homeowners to prepare soil. You can rent motor-driven rotary tillers from tool and garden centers or you can purchase one if you do a lot of gardening.

Prepare soil by using a rotary tiller. Set blades to dig down to a depth of 6–8 in. Make at least two passes before adding amendments. If your site has grass on it, set blades to a depth of 2–3 in. Rake up grass before tilling to the required depth.

# Amending Soils

## Soil Conditioners

It is a rare property that has ideal soil; therefore, amendments are needed to improve your soil. Once you have determined what kind of soil you have, you will know what to look for in an amendment.

If your soil is sandy, add organic matter to increase moisture retention and aeration. Use compost, peat moss or well-rotted manure. Avoid slower decaying materials, such as ground-up bark or sawdust—as they decompose, they will consume most of the soil's nitrogen, causing mushrooms to grow in your lawn.

To improve the texture and drainage of dense, clay soils, add almost any material that creates air spaces and breaks up the compacted clay. Sand or organic matter are best. Organic materials may be purchased at your local nursery. If you don't have a compost pile, it's a good idea to start one; compost is an excellent soil conditioner.

Adding organic matter improves the texture of the soil and greatly improves drainage. Heavy clay soil will be opened up and lighter. Sandy soil needs organic matter to retain moisture and nutrients normally leached quickly through the sand. A minimum of 30 percent of the total soil volume should be organic matter. Add enough conditioners so that you physically change the structure of the top six to eight inches of soil, the depth of most grass roots.

Determine your soil type and add the necessary amendments to make it loam. Add fertilizer and lots of organic matter such as compost, peat moss or well-rotted manure.

**Adding Amendments**

**First** Transport organic material to the site and spread evenly over soil.

**Next** Till the organic material to mix the amendment with the soil over entire surface.

**Last** Rake and level surface in preparation for planting.

# Lime and Sulfur

The application of lime or sulfur accelerates the decay of organic material, releasing essential nutrients for growth.

**Lime pellets** Granular and coarse, slower acting than ground lime.

**Finely ground lime** Has smaller particles and works faster than pellets.

**Sulfur** Comes in a powder form and works quickly.

## Applying Lime or Sulfur

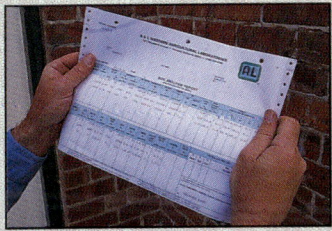

Test your soil to determine need. For best results, take a soil sample to your Agricultural Extension Service for a detailed report.

Spread lime or sulfur with spreader.

Mix with soil and water for new lawns. Water only for established lawns.

## ADJUSTING pH

Most grasses prefer a pH around 6.0–6.5, and anything outside of this range indicates an imbalance. The pH reading of your soil sample will determine the amount of lime or sulfur needed to correct the pH levels.

Acid soils are common in the humid, temperate regions of East and along the northern Pacific coast. Soils of the drier parts of the West are usually alkaline. The acidity or alkalinity of your soil directly affects the availability of plant nutrients; only by adjustment will the soil allow fertilizer to become more soluble and thus allow the grass to use these nutrients and survive. It's a good idea to test soil annually to determine need.

Apply lime to correct acidity, or sulfur to correct alkalinity. If your pH reading is low, make annual or semi-annual applications of lime at the rate of four pounds to each 100 square feet for every point below 6.5. If pH is high, add one pound of sulfur per 100 square feet of soil.

Lime comes in ground limestone or pellet form. There are two kinds of ground limestone—high calcium lime and lime containing both calcium and magnesium. The latter is more costly and needed only if your soil test indicates low magnesium. Both will raise the pH level of your lawn. Do not apply too much lime. A gradual raising of a low pH level with lime will aid in the production of beneficial soil organisms. A sudden change due to heavy applications can reduce the efficiency of soil bacteria. You can apply lime anytime, but fall or winter are best.

Alkalinity can be corrected by annual or semi-annual applications of sulfur, either in the pure yellow powder form or with a gypsum. Each application should be followed by a thorough watering.

# INSTALLING IN-GROUND IRRIGATION I

## PLANNING A SYSTEM

The advantages of an in-ground irrigation system include convenience and efficiency. Having sprinkler heads in permanent positions is easier than constantly moving around portable sprinklers. In-ground systems also eliminate uneven and inefficient water distribution—common problems with portable units. It's also a good investment, often increasing property value. The only disadvantages are the cost and installation.

Installation is not difficult, but you should shop carefully and talk to irrigation specialists, nursery people or your county extension agent. Once you have decided on a system, talk to the manufacturer's rep. Most of the time they will supply complete step-by-step instructions. Supply stores, manufacturers and garden center specialists may help you design your system. They will help you calculate the number of sprinklers and valves necessary if you provide a scale drawing of your yard.

It is essential to start with a plan. Use graph paper and make a complete plan of your property drawn to scale, making one inch for 10 feet for a small property and one inch for 20 feet or more for larger yards. Draw in lawn areas, trees and structures as well as sun, shade and slope. Plot lines and sprinklers along the perimeter of your lawn, with quarter-circle sprinkler heads in the corners, half-circle heads along the edges and full-circle heads in the middle. Overlap the spray area to ensure even coverage, working from the outside perimeter to the inside. Make a separate circuit for each area or group of sprinklers. The piping should be drawn in from the valves to the sprinklers. Avoid going under sidewalks and driveways.

Note where your water sources are for convenient hookup. Check your water pressure for GPM, gallons per minute. It is important to know this—use a gauge for greatest accuracy. Calculate the GPM for every sprinkler (flow rating should be with packaging or on a sticker). Add GPM for all the sprinklers on the line to insure the total does not exceed the GPM flow determined by the gauge; if it does, there will not be sufficient pressure to operate the system properly. Also, find out the size of the service line from your meter to the house.

Once you've planned the type and number of sprinklers you'll need, purchase pipe and components. PVC pipe is the best—use Schedule 40 PVC or class 315 for lines under constant pressure such as those leading to valves. Use less expensive class 200 for lines that will only be pressurized when the system is on. Pipe size is determined by the maximum number of GPM that can flow through. For sprinkler heads, choose adjustable, pop-up heads that remain at soil level below mower height when not in use. A pop-up height of two inches is needed for high-cut, cool-season grasses.

Dig trenches a minimum of 8–12 inches deep either by hand or with a trenching machine. Cut pipe sections to length and lay out the whole system in the trenches with loose joints before applying any glue. When everything fits correctly, join pipes with primer and glue. Next, install sprinkler risers. Then build the manifold and tap into the main service line, as described on the opposite page. Before attaching the sprinkler heads, flush the system of dirt and debris by running water through it.

In areas with freezing temperatures, be sure to install a self-draining valve at the lowest part of each circuit as well as at the lowest part of the system near the water meter.

Prior to installation, turn off the water at the meter. Cut the supply line and install a compression tee and a shutoff or gate valve. This will allow you to turn off water to the system independently, leaving the supply line to the house undisturbed. Be sure to use Teflon tape or pipe compound for water-tight connections.

An anti-siphon valve on every circuit prevents water backflow from sprinkler lines into the household water supply. Each valve will control a separate group of sprinklers. All the anti-siphon valves are placed together in a *manifold*. Each is connected to the main water supply for the system on one side, and to the pipes going out to the circuit on the other.

## CONTROL VALVE AND CONNECTIONS

It is important to note that you will never use the same sprinkler circuit to water different kinds of plants, lawn and groundcovers. Your system will need to be divided into circuits which operate one at a time. Because in many cases there will not be enough water pressure to water the entire lawn at once, each circuit will have to have a separate control valve, operated manually or electrically by an automatic timer. All the control valves are placed together in a *manifold,* with each connected on one side to its circuit and to the main water supply line on the other. The manifold should be conveniently located.

Every circuit should have an *anti-siphon valve*, which will prevent the backflow of water from draining into your household water. Most building codes require anti-siphon devices.

A *shutoff gate valve* is installed between the anti-siphon valve and the water supply connection. This enables you to turn off the entire irrigation system without losing water supply to the house.

To tap into the supply line, turn off the household water at the meter. Cut the supply pipe, and install a compression tee and shutoff valve. Follow all applicable building codes for your area. If you have a water softener, always install sprinklers between the softener and the meter. Then attach the tee to the sprinkler supply line and manifold. Use the same method to tap into the basement or existing outside faucet lines.

To make your system automatic, you will need to install an electric timer and automatic valves that turn the sprinklers on and off. The automatic valve on each circuit is managed by a control clock, which can be set to your specifications. Locate the control clock where it is protected from inclement weather.

# Installing In-Ground Irrigation II

**First** Use a pressure gauge (available from rental centers, irrigation or plumbing stores, or lawn dealers) to determine the PSI (pressure per square inch) and the GPM (gallons per minute). This information is necessary for planning your system. PSI should be at least 40. A typical GPM is 12.

**Third** Consult with a lawn center or irrigation specialist or the manufacturer's rep in your area. Select the valves, sprinklers and connectors needed for each circuit. Buy enough pipe for each line including connections to and from the valves. Also purchase Teflon tape or pipe joint compound, primer, glue and glue remover for your hands.

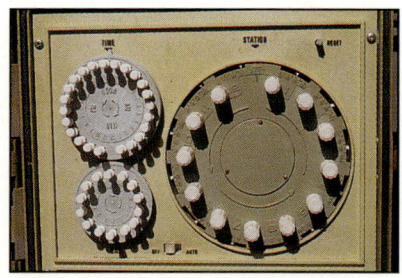

**Fifth** Install an automatically-controlled time clock if you are not using a manual system. Use direct burial or approved wire suitable for outdoor use. Time clock instructions will recommend the proper gauge for the wire and tell you how to connect to the valves and mount your clock indoors.

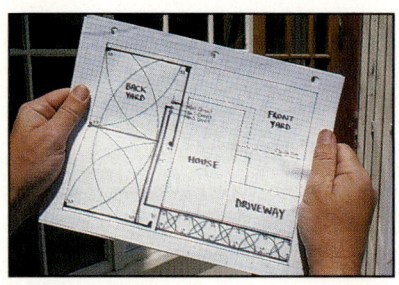

**Then** Map a system or have an irrigation specialist or sprinkler manufacturer design your irrigation system. Some supply centers will do this for free. Draw coverage areas with overlapping or head-to-head spray for even water distribution. Verify that the GPM required by each sprinkler on the circuit does not add up to more than the GPM available at the supply source.

**Fourth** Dig a trench, assemble the shutoff valves and the anti-siphon valves in the manifold and check for leaks. Remember that the pipes leading from the anti-siphon valves out to the circuit lines need to extend below ground level, since this begins the underground installation.

**Sixth** Mark your system using stakes and string according to the dimensions on the plan. Show where both lines and sprinklers go. Make sure the sprinkler heads are placed exactly as they have been drawn; if they are off, you may end up with uneven coverage.

34

**Seventh** Dig V-shaped trenches approximately 8 in. deep, or deeper if you have larger pop-up sprinklers. Use a flat-edged spade, or for large installations a trenching machine. These are available at rental centers and can save you considerable time and work.

**Ninth** Lay pipe in trenches, leaving 2–3 in. of space near any pavement or walks. Install risers if required by your system. Open the valves to flush out any dirt or debris that could clog sprinklers.

**Next** Turn the sprinklers on and test for coverage. Turn the sprinkler canister or adjust with a special key to make sure the spray arc is properly aimed. Adjust the distance of the throw of water with a screwdriver. Be sure all areas receive adequate spray.

**Eighth** Assemble the system, circuit by circuit, by laying out the pipes and cutting them with a hacksaw or PVC cutter. Remove any spurs or debris. Dry-fit the pipes first, then join them permanently using primer and solvent. Apply to both the inside of the connectors and to the outside of the pipe. Push the pipe in to seat it, rotate it 1/4 turn and let it set.

**Then** Adjust pop-up heads to required level. They should be flush or just below ground level when not in use. See that they are vertical, and not leaning so that when they pop up the spray will be uniform.

**Last** When you are satisfied with the coverage and operation of your system, backfill the trenches. Tamp down the dirt, let it settle, and add more if necessary. Replant with seed or sod.

Check that local codes allow use of PVC pipes.

# Analyzing Your Grass Needs

## Sun

Most grasses require at least six hours of sun a day. There are many varieties available for sunny areas; consider first how your lawn will be used. The general, all-purpose lawn is the most common. If you prefer an elegant, fine-bladed lawn, it will require extra care. Sturdy varieties are best for heavy traffic and families with children and pets. Also available are mixtures for difficult terrain and poor soil.

In northern or mountainous areas, bluegrass is the the most popular choice for sunny lawns. Look for mixtures containing approximately 50 percent bluegrass, 30 percent fine fescue, and 20 percent perennial ryegrass. Kentucky bluegrass and its improved varieties form a beautiful turf that wears well. They grow primarily in the spring and fall, and tend to go partially dormant in extreme hot weather. Perennial ryegrass and fescue varieties are more heat and drought tolerant. Combining them with bluegrass will provide you with an attractive lawn all summer.

If you live in the mid-South, improved turf-type tall fescues will provide an outstanding lawn in full sun. These improved varieties are superior to Kentucky 31 in color, disease resistance, texture and have a shorter growth habit. Improved varieties stand up to the hot summers and cool winters of the transition zone. Look for mixtures containing at least 70 percent turf-type tall fescue, or plant a tall fescue blend.

Bermudagrass, St. Augustine grass and the improved turf-type tall fescues are the best for sunny, southern lawns. Overseeding with a perennial ryegrass will provide you with a green lawn year-round.

## Drought

Recent concerns about conservation have prompted more and more interest in grass and plants that require little watering and that are resistant to high temperatures.

Restrictions on water usage, especially in the West, and a movement to conserve water have made us all more conscious of the amount of water we consume. Time is another consideration. It takes far less effort to maintain your lawn if the grass is a drought-tolerant variety rather than one that requires regular soakings.

Improved turf-type tall fescues are extremely drought tolerant, and many varieties will adapt to a wide range of soil types. Bermudagrass varieties do well in long hot summers and require minimum care. Improved zoysiagrass varieties are also a good choice. Improved turf-type tall fescues are long-lasting and can withstand extreme summer heat as well as winter cold. Most of the perennial ryegrasses are heat and cold tolerant as well. Check the climate map of turfgrasses (see pgs. 64–65) for the best grasses for your area.

## Shade

There are several degrees of shade—light, medium and full. Because grasses need some sun to grow, most grasses will not grow in full or deep shade. For deep shade under trees such as maples and beeches, you are better off planting a groundcover. But several grasses will grow under trees with loose open leaves in dappled or filtered shade, where the sun hits intermittently. And, of course, most grasses grow in light or medium shade, where they get sun at least part of the day.

Establishing a lawn in shade requires that you choose a shade-tolerant grass. The fine-leaved fescues, such as hard, creeping and chewings fescues, are long-lived and tolerate a fair amount of shade and dryness. Use commercially available shade mixtures for wooded areas, under trees and around shrubs, along fence lines and northern sides of buildings.

In the North, look for mixtures containing approximately 70 percent fine fescue and 50 percent shade-tolerant bluegrass varieties. The bluegrass will help to give a smooth transition from sun to shade. In shady lawns in western states, look for mixtures containing about 50 percent fine fescue, 25 percent shade-tolerant bluegrass and 25 percent rough-stalk bluegrass (or *Poa trivialis*). In the South, both St. Augustine grass and Bermudagrass perform beautifully in the shade.

## Wearability

Lawns for families with children and pets who romp and play during the summer months need to be tough and rugged. No grass is indestructible, but there are a number of grasses that can withstand rough treatment and many newer varieties that have been bred especially for this purpose.

Most of the fine fescues can take considerable punishment. They are tough and can endure shade and limited water and fertilizer.

Improved turf-type tall fescues make excellent, long-lasting lawn grasses. They mow cleanly, do not use too much water and withstand summer heat and traffic.

Special mixtures of bluegrass, fescues and improved ryegrasses can withstand heavy traffic and require little maintenance. In addition to the fescue mixtures, there is also Bermudagrass, which is deep-rooted and tough enough to stand up to heavy traffic.

Ask at your local nursery for other lawn grasses durable enough to withstand the punishment of frisky pets, romping children and adult sports and suitable for your particular climate.

# Seed, Sod, Plug or Sprig?

When planting a new lawn, you can choose to grow lawn grasses in a variety of ways: from seed, sod, plug or sprig. Consider each option to choose the right method for planting your lawn.

**Seed** Sowing seeds is easy and the most popular and inexpensive way to start a new lawn. Commercially available seed offers the greatest variety, specialty blends and mixes. Should you choose to start your lawn with seed, use the highest quality seed available. Spending a few extra dollars now will provide you with the best possible lawn later. Choose high-quality seed from a reputable company.

Seeding is the most economical way to start a new lawn. Seed costs much less than sod, sprigs or plugs. Starting a lawn from seed gives you control to plant the best type of grass for your light and soil conditions and intended use.

**Sod** The fastest way to install a new lawn is to lay sod. In fact, sod provides results as quickly as you can unroll the lush, green rolls of living carpet on your prepared soil surface. With proper watering, the root system will be fully established within two weeks.

Laying sod is popular due to its ease of installation and instant results. It is preferred for installation on steep slopes, run-off areas and other hard-to-seed areas. One disadvantage is that it's more expensive than seed, often costing 4–5 times as much as a seeded lawn and the selection of varieties may be limited. Unless you have access to a truck, you'll need to have your sod order delivered and be ready to plant immediately.

Don't be fooled by thick rolls of sod. You can't lay sod on top of existing lawn or soil. Sod won't take root through established vegetation. Soil must be prepared thoroughly to ensure the life of the sod. Sod requires the same degree of frequent waterings as a newly seeded lawn.

**Plugs** Many warm-season grasses, such as St. Augustine grass or centipedegrass, do not produce viable seed. Consequently, the grasses are sold in plugs for installation. Cool-season grasses are usually not available in plugs or sprigs.

Plugs are small 2–4 in. squares or circles of grass cut from sod with soil attached. They are "plugged" into soil at intervals of 6–12 in. in a checkerboard fashion. This is done with a plugging tool that looks very much like a bulb planter. After fertilizing the area and digging the holes, set the plugs in upright and keep well watered. In 3–6 months, depending upon the type of grass and how much you plant, the plugs will grow together to form a lawn. One disadvantage to plugs is the amount of time it will take before the lawn is established; initially, it can be unsightly.

The majority of warm-season grasses grow by spreading. Plugs have lateral stems, or stolons, that crawl along the surface and root, sending up new growth at each rooting. Plugs are easier to handle than sprigs, but cost more. However, they are not as expensive as sod.

**Sprigs** Like plugs, many southern grasses, such as Bermudagrass, zoysiagrass and centipedegrass, are planted by sprigs. Sprigs are individual stems or pieces of stems that grow by rhizomes or stolons, either across the surface or underground. Sprigs usually consist of sections of shredded stems and roots 3–6 in. long. They need at least 2–4 nodes on each stem from which roots can develop. Sprigs can be scattered over the soil like seed or planted in shallow furrows.

Sprigs should be planted according to their rate of growth. St. Augustine grass, centipedegrass and Bermudagrass sprigs should be spaced at 12-in. intervals; zoysiagrass, which grows more slowly, at 6-in. intervals.

Soil preparation and post-planting care are virtually the same as for plugs. The soil should be ready so the sprigs can be planted as soon as they arrive. Sprigs should never be left to dry out; this is crucial to establishing sprigs. Sprigs are a bit more difficult to handle than plugs but are less expensive.

It is important that sprigs are firmly pressed into the soil to establish roots. Use a roller twice, once after planting, and a second time after topdressing. In hot, dry, or windy weather, do not plant entire lawn before watering; sprigs will need water within 2–3 hours of planting. Water with a fine spray promptly after planting is completed; keep moist for at least 10 days.

# Choosing Grass Mixtures

## Specialty Mixes

Turfgrass specialists recommend sowing a mixture of lawn grass varieties to produce a healthy, attractive home lawn.

Preformulated specialty mixes are available at your local garden center, or you can formulate your own mix by purchasing individual varieties and combining them yourself. By adjusting the amounts of bluegrass, perennial ryegrass, and fescue in your seed mixture, you can develop a custom mix to meet the exact needs of your lawn.

Improved varieties of Kentucky bluegrass are considered the premier turfgrasses. Their characteristic blue-green color and fine texture are the hallmark of showcase front lawns. Bluegrass requires high fertility and plenty of water, and is best suited to northern climates or areas where irrigation is accessible. New varieties have been bred for better disease resistance. Most bluegrass varieties are not shade tolerant nor drought tolerant. Include bluegrass in your mix for beauty. Use more than one bluegrass variety if more than 25 percent of your lawn seed mixture will be bluegrass.

Perennial ryegrasses have been improved to blend well with other popular turfgrass varieties. Their deep root systems grow down into the soil and tap ground moisture, making them drought and traffic tolerant. Aggressive root systems also loosen the soil, making it easier for less sturdy grasses to take root and establish. Add perennial ryegrass to your mix if you have poor soil and dry conditions. Perennial ryegrasses are great for overseeding to renew aging lawns.

Fine fescues are the turfgrasses that perform well in sun or shade. They are also drought and traffic tolerant. Their fine texture and versatility make them invaluable in any lawn seed mix. Fine fescues are usually combined with bluegrass to make a sun and shade mix.

Improved turf-type tall fescues are quickly becoming one of the best components for a custom home lawn seed mixture. Improved fescues are drought tolerant and relatively disease free. The plants are quick to establish, requiring minimum fertility and mixture. Turf-type tall fescue lawns are low maintenance, requiring less fertilizing, watering and mowing than bluegrass or perennial ryegrass. Add them to your mix if you want an easy-care lawn.

## Benefits of Mixtures and Blends

Although you can purchase grass seed for a single variety, most seed is now sold in mixtures or blends. The reasons are practical. *Mixtures* contain different varieties of seed that adjust to different growing conditions. One kind may be more adaptable to sun, another to shadier areas. No single type of grass is likely to suit every part of the lawn. By planting a mixture of grasses you are, in effect, planting different grasses for each area. Also, a planting of a single grass could be wiped out should disease strike. If you have a good selection of grasses the most adaptable and vigorous will survive adverse conditions.

A premium mixture includes seeds for grasses that have a complementary color, texture and rate of growth. The grasses will also be compatible in dormancy and aggressiveness. Three types of grasses that meet these qualifications and are often mixed are bluegrass, fescue, and perennial ryegrass. By varying the amounts of bluegrass, ryegrass and fescues, you can develop a seed mixture that meets the specific needs of your lawn.

A *blend* is a combination of varieties from one type of grass. The advantage of a blend is consistency in color and texture that creates a show-piece lawn. Blending varieties also builds resistance to disease.

The term *nurse grass* usually refers to annual ryegrass, a fast-growing grass that precedes the perennial grass. Nurse grass shades and protects the perennial grass seedlings; however, a number of mixtures will include improved varieties of perennial ryegrass for quick cover. A premium mix should not include more than 20–30 percent of annual ryegrass.

# Choosing Grass Seed

## Read Your Label

Read the label carefully on the box of grass seed. Note the proportions of different types of seed if you're using a mix. There will be an analysis of ryegrass, bluegrass and fescue, and the percentage of each will be stated. Look for named varieties and improved varieties of grasses. For example, an improved variety of turf-type tall fescue is 'Amigo.' A blend is more than one variety of a single type of grass; for example, 'Amigo', 'Arriba' and 'Arid' is a blend of improved turf-type tall fescues.

The "Other Ingredients" list on the label also provides critical information. Weed seed is impossible to keep totally out of any mix, but look for less than one percent. "Crop seeds" means any commercially grown crop and can be problematic; buy zero or as close to zero as possible. Quality seed should contain no noxious weeds. Inert matter, dirt and miscellaneous matter should total less than four percent.

| SEEDING RATE | | | Net Wt . 5Lbs. |
|---|---|---|---|
| Overseeding Thin Lawns | | | 1 lb. per 700 sq. ft |
| New Lawns | | | 1 lb. per 350 sq. ft |

**FAST & FINE GRASS SEED MIXTURE**

| PURE SEED | KIND | GERM | ORGIN |
|---|---|---|---|
| 29.25% | Kelly Kentucky Bluegrass | 85.00% | Oregon |
| 29.10% | Creeping Red Fescue* | 85.00% | Oregon |
| 19.20% | Dandy Perennial Ryegrass | 85.00% | Oregon |
| 19.20% | Pennfine Perennial Ryegrass | 85.00% | Oregon |
| 0.96% | Crop Seed | | |
| 2.12% | Inert Matter | | |
| 0.17% | Weed Seed | | |

NOXIOUS WEEDS: NONE  Test Date: 4-92
*Variety not stated  IN CALIFORNIA ONLY SELL BY: 7-93
LOT NO: 47511-20821234  Packed by N.K. LAWN & GARDEN CO.
P.O. Box 50282, Mpls., MN 55459

## CHOOSING SEED

Quality counts in grass seed. Quality seed should be free of noxious weeds and have a high rate of germination. Purchase seed from a reputable company—spending a few extra cents to ensure a healthy lawn at the outset could save you a tidy sum in headaches and dollars down the road.

Choose seed that grows well in your area. Acquaint yourself with the types of grass that perform best in your climate. If you are unsure, consult your local nursery. Read seed labels carefully, as outlined on the opposite page.

If you are purchasing a package of a single type of seed—that is, not mixed or blended seed—be sure that the label reads at least 90 percent pure. This means that 90 percent of the material is whole seed with only 10 percent inert matter. It is virtually impossible to produce 100 percent pure seed.

Premium lawn seed is sold in cartons or bags in quantities from one to 50 pounds. You can purchase just the amount you need to repair bare spots or to seed your entire lawn. The coverage and seedling rate should be clearly stated on the package. Reputable companies will also point out the features and benefits of the mix on the package, making it easier for you to determine which mix is the best for your lawn. Beware of "all-purpose" mixes.

For permanent, perennial lawns, check the analysis label for the amount of perennial versus annual grasses. Premium mixtures will not contains more than 10 percent annual ryegrass. Mixes containing a large percentage of annual ryegrass may be used for quick cover or winter overseeding.

When choosing seed, look for a high germination rate, that is, the percentage of seed that will germinate under ideal conditions.

# Planting Lawns From Seed

Prepare soil thoroughly prior to planting seeds by determining your soil needs and adding amendments and fertilizer. Remember, the success of the your lawn depends on good soil preparation.

**Seeding a Lawn**

**First** Grading should be complete and soil should be prepared properly with the lawn area raked smooth and level.

**Then** Seed can be sown with the same kind of spreader used to distribute fertilizer. Spread around the perimeters first, then walk back and forth in rows. Make a second pass at a right angle to the first pass to assure proper coverage.

**Third** Rake the seed to cover it with 1/8–1/4 in. of soil. Rake gently so seed is not redistributed. Roll soil surface to keep seeds intact and from blowing away.

**Last** For best results, add a light mulch of compost, peat or straw to keep the soil moist and to aid germination. Water with fine spray 1–3 times a day until established.

## SEEDING TIPS

Prior to planting, complete soil preparation and surface grade. Loosen the top half inch of soil to allow for seed coverage. Soil clods or lumps of one-half to one inch are all right and help keep the soil from crusting.

Sow seed as evenly as possible. Use a drop spreader, the same one you use to spread fertilizer, sowing in rows and slightly overlapping rows to ensure even spread. You can also sow seed with a hand-held broadcast spreader. The spreader holds about three pounds of seeds; sow by walking rows approximately three to four feet apart. For smaller areas you can distribute seed by hand. It is more difficult to get even distribution, but it can be done. Divide the amount of seed to be sown in half. Spread half the seed in one direction, then spread the second half at right angles across the first half, applying the second half of seed directly over the first.

For even coverage, don't sow seed on a windy day. Never spread seed on wet soil, which can become compacted and hinder germination. The best times for seeding your lawn are fall and spring. Seeding in late summer or early fall is preferred for cool-season grasses because the temperatures are still warm enough to promote rapid germination and rainfall is plentiful. Cooler temperatures and shorter days are ideal for development and growth of young seedlings. Spring is the next best time, but there will be much more competition from germinating weed seed. Late spring is the best time to establish a warm-season lawn from seed. Planting both cool- and warm-season grasses in mid summer is difficult because of seasonal high temperatures, modest rainfall and peak weed growth.

# Planting Lawns from Sod

## Instant Results

Sod is growing turf purchased at a nursery or directly from a sod farm. It usually comes in strips six feet long, 18-24 inches wide and one inch thick. You install it much the same way you lay down carpet inside your house. The sod strips can be cut easily with a knife to fit snugly around sprinklers, sidewalks, fences and flower beds. Once laid, the sod forms an instant, living carpet of lawn.

To install sod, you need to know the square footage of your lawn. Measure the lawn areas only; exclude the house, drive and other structures. To calculate square footage, multiply the width by the length. For example, a lawn area 50 feet wide by 80 feet long measures 4,000 square feet. If your lawn has unusual shapes, calculate area for distinct sections separately, then add the measurements to compute the total area.

Use care when you purchase sod. Don't buy it if the grass is yellowing or the turf has large cracks in it; these are signs that it hasn't been watered correctly. Check carefully for any signs of insects or disease. The grass should be thick and have good color with no weeds. Many states require "certified" sod, which will be guaranteed—be sure to ask.

Sod can be laid at nearly any time of the year except during freezing weather; however, it is best to avoid the intense heat of mid summer. Sod is available in both warm-season and cool-season grasses, but you will have fewer varieties to choose from than you have with seed.

Nurseries and contractors purchase sod from a sod farm such as the one shown here.

## Sodding

**First** Prepare the soil thoroughly. Add soil amendments; apply fertilizers to the entire surface. Water well. Sod may be laid directly on the fertilizer.

**Third** For steep slopes and runoff areas, stake the sod in place with wooden pegs or sod pins to hold sod temporarily. Lay sod pieces horizontally.

**Then** Start laying sod from the back of property to the front. Fit strips tightly, avoiding gaps, making sure that each piece has good contact with soil. Use a sharp knife to cut around any obstacles.

**Last** Press sod into soil bed with half-filled water roller to ensure good contact between the soil and sod. Make 3 separate passes. Keep constantly moist for at least 10 days.

# Planting Lawns from Sprigs and Plugs

A common method of establishing lawns in the warmer regions of the country is to plant sprigs or plugs of a variety of grasses. The sprigs and plugs grow and spread quickly and soon knit together to form an entire lawn.

Before planting your lawn, measure the number of square feet in your lawn, adding about a 10 percent allowance when you order your sprigs or plugs. Choose appropriate sprigs or plugs for your area.

## Sprigging

**First** Till the soil with a rotary tiller, then add amendments and fertilizers. Smooth surface. Water lightly.

**Next** Scatter sprigs evenly at 1 bushel per 200 sq. ft. Roll surface with roller.

**Last** Cover lightly with organic matter. Roll area again. Water well with a fine spray. Keep moist at all times for at least 10 days.

**Plugging**

**First** Cut checkerboard pattern of holes with a plugging tool every 6–12 in. Sprinkle balanced fertilizer over entire lawn.

**Last** Set each plug in hole, then press firmly. Keep constantly moist with a fine spray of water.

# WARM-SEASON GRASSES

Sprigs (also called "stolons") and plugs are commonly used to build lawns in the South and Southwest. Warm-season grasses, such as Bermudagrass, carpetgrass, centipedegrass, St. Augustine grass and zoysiagrass, are much more often planted with these pieces of growing grass than from seed. Many of these grasses may not breed true from seed and some do not produce viable seed at all. All sprigged and plugged grasses spread by moving along the surface or underground by stolons or rhizomes, often called "runners." Both sprigs and plugs are best planted in spring.

Sprigs contain both leaves and roots. They can be purchased already separated by the bushel, or you can buy sod and cut out sprigs yourself. One bushel should be enough to plant 200 square feet. They often arrive within 24 hours of your order; order only when you are ready to plant. Keep sprigs moist. Scatter sprigs evenly, or plant sprigs in furrowed rows, 6–12 inches apart. You can also press them into the soil 6–8 inches apart around your lawn. The sprigs will look a bit sparse at first, but will grow together in three to six months, depending on the grass type and how close you plant them. The more sprigs you plant, the quicker your lawn will grow in.

Plugs are small, two to four inch squares or circles of grass with soil attached cut from sod. Plugs have lateral stems, or stolons, that crawl and root along the surface, creating new shoots with each rooting. They are best planted in intervals around the lawn and they will grow together in approximately three to six months. As with sprigs, soil should be prepared ahead of time. A topdressing of compost or organic matter is usually recommended to keep rains from washing away the soil.

# Watering

Watering methods differ for various kinds of lawns. This is especially true for new lawns. Proper watering is critical just after planting or installation. Pay careful attention to the needs of your lawn to ensure its healthy establishment.

## Watering after Seeding

Watering incorrectly is the most common cause of failure for newly seeded lawns. Keep moist at all times until established and rope off the area to prevent foot traffic on the lawn.

- Soak thoroughly after sowing. Avoid puddling or excessive runoff.
- Keep soil consistently damp at all times.
- Give two to three light sprinklings a day, more if necessary, until established. It's better to sprinkle lightly than to saturate.
- Water more frequently if hot or windy.
- Water with fine mist spray.
- Note germination time and rate of growth; keep track of time.
- If necessary, keep a light mulch on lawn to keep moisture in and to prevent erosion from heavy rains.
- If using portable sprinklers, set them up when you plant the lawn and leave in place until the seedlings are one and one-half to two inches high.
- Use a sprinkler that applies water as slowly and gently as possible. Run sprinkler until puddles just begin to form.

Follow these procedures for four to six weeks until root system is established.

## Watering after Sodding

Watering is the most important step after installation in establishing the root system of your sod. Water carefully. The heavy soil matrix that holds sod together does not absorb water readily.

- Water soil thoroughly one to two days before installing.
- Soak to a minimum of six inches to encourage rapid, deep root growth. Water until the sod is squishy wet.
- Water deeply, twice daily if necessary, for the first 10–14 days.
- Lift a corner of the sod to be sure water is penetrating deeply.
- Areas near driveways and paths will dry out the fastest and be the slowest to establish. Water these edges more frequently, if possible.
- Pay careful attention that water is penetrating deeply and not running off of sections on slopes and run-off areas.

## WATERING AFTER SPRIGGING AND PLUGGING

Sprigs and plugs are extremely vulnerable to drying out. If you cannot plant them immediately after receiving them, keep them moist and in a shaded location and plant as soon as possible.

- Soil should be slightly moist before planting.
- Water sections of sprigs or stolons as you plant them.

### For Sprigs

- Keep consistently moist, watering daily, if necessary. Never let sprigs and stolons dry out.
- Continue watering at frequent intervals for three to six months until the sprigs have grown together.

### For Plugs

- Water the entire section as soon as you've finished planting.
- Continue liberal waterings of plugs for two to three months, keeping moist until established.

## WATERING ESTABLISHED LAWNS

Water is vital to maintaining your lawn. Knowing when and how much to water your lawn is fundamental to its survival.

All areas of your lawn should receive equal amounts of water. Check by placing equal-sized containers in a grid pattern around your lawn. Start a timer, then turn on your watering system. After 15 minutes, check the water depth in each container. Each should hold approximately the same amount of water. If there's more than a one-quarter inch difference between the containers, adjust or change your sprinklers. Test again and keep adjusting with each watering until the system waters your lawn evenly. Use the amount collected in 15 minutes to tell how long to water to apply one inch of water to the whole lawn.

The slope and grade of your lawn is also important. Water will run off a lawn that is sloped too much. One that is uneven will puddle with wet and dry areas.

Soil probes that measure soil moisture can help you determine how much moisture is reaching the roots of your grass. Most lawn centers have several models for every price range and desired feature.

Unless you live in an arid region with sandy soil, there is no reason to water every single day. This is a waste of water. Plant a drought-tolerant grass type to conserve water. Under normal conditions, watering once or twice weekly should be enough. More may be needed during the hottest months. Test your soil to be sure.

# Mowing

## First Mowing

A newly planted lawn is more fragile than an established lawn. Freshly planted grass takes a few weeks to become established, so care should be taken during first mowing to avoid damage. Although roots are established after several weeks, they may not be deep enough to sustain a mowing. Reel mowers work best because they are gentle and cut cleanly. Cut after the morning dew has dried from the grass. Turn corners carefully to avoid uprooting tender grass with the wheels.

Don't be afraid to mow your new lawn. Mowing will encourage the grass to grow and help it spread.

Mow the grass when it grows one-third taller than its recommended height (see pgs. 68–75). For example, if the ideal height of your grass is two inches, then mow it when the blades first reach three inches high. Adjust your mower to cut two inches high, but no lower. Scalping your grass may kill it. It is very important that your mower be sharp; dull blades pull and rip, sometimes pulling out grass by the roots. Soil should be firm and dry when you mow. Withhold water the day before so mower wheels won't create ruts. During wet periods, hold off mowing until the soil dries out a little.

## GOOD MOWING PRACTICES

Mow established grass when it is one-third taller than the recommended height. How often to mow depends on the type of grass, how much you fertilize and water it and the season. Grass doesn't grow at the same rate all year round. For example, in cool-season areas, bluegrass may need cutting twice a week in peak rainfall times of spring and fall but only every other week during the summer. Frequent watering and fertilizing promotes vigorous growth.

Don't cut on a time schedule. Instead, match your mowing times to the lawn's growth. Cutting to the right height encourages healthy growth and disease and pest tolerance, reducing the need for care or pesticides.

Lawn mowers are either rotary or reel type. Rotary mower blades spin horizontally and are the most popular because of their low cost, durability and flexibility. For these reasons, this type is the most popular with the homeowner. Reel mowers have blades that rotate in a circle above the turf. They are expensive, but highly efficient; they cut grass cleanly and are used on golf courses, putting greens and large residential and commercial lawns.

Hand-pushed, non motorized reel mowers are quieter, lighter and less expensive than power reel mowers. They are easy to handle and use no energy except your own. They are an excellent choice for the small lawn.

Use common sense when operating a power mower, and keep safety in mind. Always turn off the mower and disconnect the spark plug when unclogging blades or parts; wear heavy shoes to protect feet and long pants to protect legs from muffler or engine burns; stop the engine when unattended and keep away from children.

# FERTILIZING

## HOW TO CHOOSE FERTILIZERS

When new grass plants have been mowed two to three times, apply lawn fertilizer to further stimulate their development. Regular applications of a complete fertilizer are necessary to establish and maintain a good lawn.

Fertilizers—whether for new lawns or established lawns—are usually labeled with three numbers, such as 5-10-5. Each number designates the percentage, by weight, of the nutrients nitrogen, phosphorus and potassium, or N-P-K. New lawns require a 5-10-5 mix. Established lawns need more nitrogen, less phosphorus, so select a 10-3-4 balance. Apply at the rate the label recommends.

Fertilizers are organic or inorganic. Organic fertilizers are made from the remains of plants and animals, such as blood, bone, hoof, fish and horn meal, manures and plant meal. They release nutrients slowly but are not always balanced. They may not always release their nutrients during the growing season of your turfgrasses. Inorganic fertilizers are manufactured from minerals. They release nutrients quickly, giving immediate results.

Both types come in dry and liquid forms. Dry fertilizers dissolve with each watering and may release nutrients for two to three months. Liquids are applied with a hose-end sprayer. They start to work immediately but they do not last long and are generally more expensive.

### Applying Dry Lawn Fertilizer

**First** Determine coverage rate, choose and purchase fertilizer. If necessary, rent a spreader from your local lawn and garden center and discuss how to adjust spreader flow to assure proper coverage for your lawn.

**Then** Applying fertilizer with a drop spreader is best for a small lawn. Set the spreader setting to half the label recommended rate. Apply in parallel rows, overlapping wheel tracks.

**Third** Apply a second pass of fertilizer at right angles. Use a broadcast spreader for medium or large lawns. Distribute along the outer perimeters first, then walk parallel rows, overlapping slightly for an even spread.

**Last** Water the lawn thoroughly with a fine spray to dampen and activate the fertilizer.

# APPLYING LAWN FERTILIZER

Apply fertilizer by one of three methods: broadcast spreading, drop spreading or liquid spraying. Hand-casting is not recommended.

Broadcast spreading is fast and efficient. Use a hand-operated or walk-behind applicator to throw dry fertilizer from a hopper onto the lawn. Be sure to apply in a two-step crisscross pattern, using half-rate application with each step for full coverage.

Although slower than broadcast spreading, drop spreading is recommended for applying dry fertilizer. The walk-behind spreader drops an even amount of fertilizer across the lawn. Drop spreaders can be purchased or rented from lawn centers. Adjust the outlet flow, following fertilizer or spreader label instructions, or ask for advice from your lawn center.

Visually check that you applied the fertilizer evenly. Always overlap wheel tracks to avoid missing areas. Uneven fertilization causes ragged growth and may burn your lawn. If necessary, spread it further with a garden rake and water the fertilizer after each application.

Liquid fertilizers are applied by using a garden hose-end sprayer. The fertilizer container will tell you the fertilizer-to-water mix. Before you begin spraying, determine the midpoint of your lawn and use only half the liquid fertilizer by the time you reach it. Liquid fertilizers can burn if applied in too strong a concentration.

Different grasses have different fertilizer requirements. Fertilize bluegrass three times per year; fescues and perennial ryegrass need two yearly applications. If you can only fertilize once, fall is the best time, when grass is storing food.

# ANNUAL MAINTENANCE

## WEED AND PEST CONTROL

The best weed control method is prevention. Proper mowing, fertilizing, watering, dethatching and aerating all help to keep weeds to a minimum.

Weeds come in two types: grass or broadleafed. Grass weeds are simply grasses other than the type you want growing in your lawn. Broadleafed weeds are all non-grass weeds. They are easier to identify than grass weeds and are usually easy to pull by hand. Pre-emergent and post-emergent herbicides, respectively, are used to destroy weeds before and after they appear. Use with great care and only as directed; healthy lawns usually do not need these treatments.

Moss, algae and mushrooms plague lawns with poor drainage, too much watering, lack of light, fertilizer or air circulation. These can be pulled or raked out.

Harmful lawn pests come in three groups: those that live above ground and feed on grass fluids; those that live on the soil surface and feed on leaves and crowns; and those that live underground and eat grass roots. While pests can damage your lawn, remember that many harmless or helpful insects also live there. Most harmful insects can be controlled through good lawn maintenance.

Lawn diseases caused by various types of fungi can turn your lawn brown in a matter of days. Because diseases are encouraged by poor lawn care, control thatch and water and fertilize properly to avoid turning your lawn into a haven for disease.

The most common weeds are featured to the right.

### Dandelion
*Taraxacum officinale*
This common weed grows over most of the world. Its yellow flower has a very long taproot that must be dug out. Remove before it goes to seed.

### Crabgrass
*Digitaria sanguinalis*
An annual grass that spreads out flat from the center and is almost impossible to get a hold of without a tool. Grows in any soil. Must be dug out.

### Spotted Spurge
*Euphorbia maculata*
Looks like clover but small green leaves have a small red spot near the center and grow from white or red stalks. Appears in spring and grows until fall.

### Oxalis
*Oxalis corniculata*
Small, clover-like leaves are green or purple and grow from a shallow taproot. Its spring pods explode to toss seeds nearly 6 ft. Easy to pull out.

### Plantain
*Plantago* species
A cool-season weed that grows in spring and fall. Oval-shaped leaves form rosettes up to 6 in. across. Slender flower stalk curls at the top.

### Quackgrass
*Agropyron repens*
Spreads rapidly by underground stolons or by seeds. Remove early, before seeds set. Be careful—every piece will regenerate a new plant.

# FALL LAWN CARE

Although several chores, such as mowing and weeding, are done throughout the year, some specific lawn chores are usually saved for the fall.

**Fertilize** A fall application of fertilizer supplies the nutrients critical for grass to form deep roots and store food for growth for the next season.

**Lime** If your soil is acidic, liming often has the biggest impact on establishing growth. You can distribute lime any time of year, but fall is an excellent time. Use your soil test and pH ratio as your guide.

**Rake leaves** Get your leaves up as soon as possible. Do not wait until they are all down and then rake. Rain mats leaves and they can smother your grass.

**Overseed** If you have a warm-season grass that goes dormant in cool weather, you can keep the lawn green through winter by overseeding. Most cool-season grasses can be used. Annual ryegrass is inexpensive and quick-growing. Perennial ryegrasses and fescues also work well. To winter overseed, mow the lawn short, then fertilize.

**Plant** The ideal time for planting most kinds of grass is late summer or early fall. It's the best time for germination and early growth for cool-season grasses. Warm-season grasses can be started in spring.

**Watering** Although the heaviest watering may be done during warm summer months, be sure your lawn also is watered well before going dormant to keep the roots from dying out.

# Long-Term Maintenance

Sooner or later your lawn will need some kind of renovation. There is no set timetable showing when thatch will build up or soil will become compacted. But proper maintenance practices will extend the time between necessary renovation.

# THE 3-5 YEAR PLAN

Lawns occasionally thin out and become weedy as a result of poor management, pests or severe summer drought. Even the best manicured lawns can lose their sheen.

Unlike the seasonal chores of mowing, fertilizing and watering, renovation is done on an as-needed basis, sometimes annually but usually every 3-5 years.

How often you will need to dethatch will depend on the type of grass you have and how often you fertilize. Thatch—the buildup of decaying plant debris at the turf base—is primarily a problem of intensely fertilized and watered lawns. Remove clippings to deter thatch buildup and fertilize and water less frequently. Fertilizing once a year, complemented by proper watering practices, should reduce the need to dethatch from an annual cycle to once every 3-5 years.

Any turfgrass that receives constant traffic, whether from sports, bikes or walking, will suffer soil compaction. Grass can't grow if water and nutrients are blocked from its roots by compacted soil. Aeration is necessary to open the soil. On a properly maintained lawn with moderate traffic, this will need to be done every 2-3 years. If you have poor soil where compaction is a constant problem, you will need to aerate every 1-2 years.

# Alternatives to Turfgrass

## Easy Care Options

Groundcovers can be decorative and practical alternatives to lawn grass. They are neat, attractive and often require substantially less maintenance. For less work and variety, consider planting groundcovers.

Grass and groundcovers work well together. Blankets of groundcovers around trees and foundations provide texture and visual interest. Most groundcovers are low growing, need very little pruning, and many are evergreen.

Groundcovers also grow on tough terrain. Grass doesn't hold well on steep slopes; groundcovers will set roots firmly and keep erosion in check. Dry, deeply shaded areas under low-branching trees will be unable to sustain grass growth but ivy, pachysandra or wild ginger will thrive. A low area in the shade that may not drain well is perfect for a mass planting of feathery ferns. A hot, dry area above a retaining wall that is difficult and dangerous to mow is ideal for periwinkle or another groundcover.

Groundcovers require very little grooming other than occasional trimming or fertilizing. They are readily planted and enjoyed. However, most groundcovers are not for walking on. With the exception of dichondra, they do not recover like grass.

**Dichondra**

*Dichondra micrantha*

Often used as a lawn substitute in warm climates. Fast-growing evergreen, up to 1 ft. Low, round-leaf groundcover that tolerates shade. Mow to 1 in. Low maintenance but needs heavy fertilization. Zones 9–10.

**Blue Fescue**

*Festuca ovina glauca*

An ornamental grass with mounds of bright blue-gray leaves. Sturdy, compact habit growing 6–12 in. high. Highly decorative as a groundcover or accent plant. Likes dry soil with good drainage. Zones 4–10.

## Pachysandra

*Pachysandra terminalis*

Also called Japanese spurge, this low-growing perennial is the most widely used of all groundcovers. It thrives under dry conditions and deep shade. Grows to 5–10 in. with evergreen foliage. Zones 3–8.

## English Ivy

*Hedera* species

An evergreen vine grown as a groundcover or a climber, growing to 6 in. on the ground. Leaves are dark green and spread by aerial roots. Grows in all conditions, average soil, sun to deep shade. Zones 5–10.

## Periwinkle

*Vinca minor*

Also known as myrtle, this hardy groundcover is fast growing, forming a trailing dense cover 6–10 in. high and 24 in. across. Numerous blue or white flowers in spring. Well-drained soil in part to deep shade. Zones 5–9.

## Winter Creeper

*Euonymus fortunei*

Hardy evergreen vine that roots as it grows along the ground, trails out to 20 ft., 12–24 in. high. Leaves turn purple in autumn and winter. Produces berries. Very easy, full sun to full shade. Zones 4–9.

# Planting Broadleaf Groundcovers

## Groundcover Alternatives

Planting groundcovers requires the same amount of advance work as planting grass. Because groundcovers are meant to last for years, soil preparation and drainage are essential.

As a rule, groundcovers should be planted in the spring. Some can be planted in the fall, but often they do not have enough time to establish their root systems before cool weather sets in. Choose plants that thrive in your area and follow specific instructions for cultivation. Find out your soil type and add the necessary amendments. Add lots of organic matter.

Although groundcovers need less maintenance, they require special care during installation. Select suitable plants and buy enough plants to cover the entire area. Make sure the plants have a good, strong root system. Soon after planting, groundcovers will begin spreading aerial roots or will send out runners to intertwine with nearby plants.

Water newly planted groundcovers regularly. Until they become established, this is very important in encouraging growth. Even drought-tolerant plants will need more water than they will when established. In addition to water, newly installed groundcovers need regular fertilizing.

Keep a careful eye out for weeds while your groundcovers are filling in. Pull weeds immediately and use a mulch.

## Planting Groundcovers

**First** Clear soil surface, dig 10–12 in. deep. Add organic material and fertilizer and turn into soil.

**Next** Dig holes with trowel in staggered rows. Set plants out by loosening roots and place in hole, keeping roots down.

**Last** Firm plant in soil and water to settle. Water regularly, soaking roots and avoiding foliage, until established.

# Climate Map of Turfgrasses

Choose the best grasses for your climate: *cool-season* (grows in cooler, northern climates, but withers in hot southern summers) or *warm-season* (flourishes in summer heat, but becomes dormant—turns brown—in chilly weather). A mix is often used in areas where summers are hot and winters are cold.

### South
Hot, moist summers, cool winters. Choose Bermudagrass, St. Augustine grass or centipedegrass. Use tall fescue and Kentucky bluegrass in higher, cooler elevations.

### Southwest
Hot, dry summers, mild winters. Pick Bermudagrass, St. Augustine grass or zoysiagrass for lower elevations, buffalograss and perennial ryegrass for higher elevations and for winter overseeding.

### Tropical
Wet and warm year round. In very wet areas, choose disease-tolerant carpetgrass. Bermudagrass, centipedegrass, bahiagrass and St. Augustine grass also do well.

### Mountain States, West Canada
Very cold winters, dry summers. Choose native grasses like buffalograss, crested wheatgrass and blue grama. For irrigated, protected areas use fescues and Kentucky bluegrass.

### Northeast, East Canada
Wet, mild summers, cold winters. Choose Kentucky bluegrass, fine fescues and perennial ryegrass.

### Transition
Both cool-season and warm-season grasses are used in mixes. Neither can adapt year round. Tall fescues provide best results.

### Midwest
Hot, humid summers, cold winters. Use bluegrass, perennial ryegrass and fescue.

### Pacific Northwest
Cool, moist climate with moderate winters. Kentucky bluegrass, fine fescues and perennial ryegrass do well.

65

# Regional Differences

## Warm and Mild Areas

Bermudagrass, buffalograss and zoysiagrass perform well in warmer areas, while improved Kentucky bluegrass and turf-type tall fescues do best in the cooler sections or higher elevations. Alkaline soils treated with iron supplements and sulfur produce best results. An excellent alternative to grass is dichondra, a broadleaf plant that behaves like a grass. It wears well and can be mowed.

Many warm areas have limited rainfall and arid conditions, making watering one of the most time-consuming lawn chores. Choose drought-tolerant grasses and install an in-ground irrigation system with automatic timers. Drought-tolerant grasses require much less water, and automatic irrigation systems will save you time.

Warm-season grasses go dormant in cool weather. Winter overseeding in late fall with annual or perennial ryegrass will establish a quick-growing, lush, green lawn for the winter months. Spring is a good time to reseed bare spots with warm-season grasses. Keep them well watered to ensure grass is established before hot weather arrives. Applying high-nitrogen fertilizer in March will help to rouse warm-season grasses out of dormancy.

Fall is the best time to do a soil test and the best time to add amendments to adjust pH. If you need to dethatch or aerate for soil compaction, fall is also a good time.

## Cold and Temperate Areas

In cooler regions, Kentucky bluegrass, fine fescues and perennial ryegrass perform best. Mixtures are also good and often preferred. Soils are acidic in the East, while in the Midwest soils range from alkaline and sandy to acidic and clay. Soil tests are important to determine appropriate amendments.

If you are adding lime to adjust soil pH, add it in the fall when grass is storing nutrients. Although lime and sulfur can be applied at any time of the year, these elements help release nutrients and so are best applied at this time.

Sowing seeds or laying sod are common practices for installing new lawns in the North since only warm-season grasses are available in sprigs and plugs. Sow seed in late summer or early fall; temperatures are ideal for germination and there is less weed competition. You can lay sod at any time, but it is best to avoid the hottest months.

Rainfall is usually adequate in temperate areas, especially in spring and fall. Summers bring sporadic precipitation, so watering will become an important chore. An in-ground system may not be needed for only a short few months, but it is a luxury that can save a lot of time.

Fall is also an important time to fertilize, to provide nutrients for the grass to store. Fertilize in early fall and continue to rake until all the leaves are up to prevent diseases, insect infestations and smothering of the grass.

Dethatching and aerating are best done in the fall but can also be done in the spring.

Transition zones between the North and the South have a wide variety of soils and microclimates. Local advice is best in choosing grasses.

# Cool-Season Grasses I

**Creeping Bentgrass**
*Agrostis stolonifera pulustris*
Creeping bentgrass produces a gorgeous lawn of fine-textured, thick and lush green turf—a high-quality, high-maintenance lawn often used on golf courses but seldom as a home lawn. Needs frequent waterings. A vigorous creeper by stolons. Tolerates a fair amount of wear and shade. Plant by seed or sprigs in fall for spring. Recommend 1–2 lbs./1,000 sq. ft. Germinates in 4–12 days. Mow to 1/4–1/2 in. high.

**Rough-Stalk Bluegrass**
*Poa trivialis*
Rough-stalk bluegrass is the most shade tolerant cool-season lawn grass. This fine-textured grass has bright, yellow-green leaves. Although lacking the toughness and cold tolerance of Kentucky bluegrass, it thrives in damp, shaded areas. Sensitive to pests and diseases. Requires more frequent waterings than Kentucky bluegrass. Plant by seed in fall or spring. Recommend 2 lbs./1,000 sq. ft. Germinates in 6–30 days. Mow 1 1/2–2 in. high.

**Common Kentucky Bluegrass**
*Poa pratensis*
The most popular cool-season grass due to its adaptability and hardiness. A premium lawn grass that produces rich green color and dense growth. Kentucky bluegrass spreads by rhizomes and is extremely hardy in cold winters. Withstands heavy foot traffic, and many varieties are disease and pest resistant. Grows best in full sun. Plant by seed or lay sod in fall or spring. Recommend 2 lbs./1,000 sq. ft. Germinates in 6–30 days. Mow 1 1/2–2 in. high.

### Improved Kentucky Bluegrass
*Poa* species

Improved hybrid varieties of Kentucky bluegrass have all of the fine qualities of common bluegrass, but most are more disease and insect resistant. Some will even tolerate low nitrogen levels, which means less fertilizing. Rich lawn grasses that produce good green color and thick growth. Spreads by rhizomes and endures heavy traffic and play. Plant by seed or lay sod in fall or spring. Recommend 2 lbs./1,000 sq. ft. Germinates in 6–30 days. Mow 1 1/2–2 in. high.

### Perennial Ryegrass
*Lolium perenne*

A very quick grower that is compatible in mixes with Kentucky bluegrass and fine fescues. A vigorous grass that has shiny, bright green leaves that remain green throughout cool weather. Frequently used to overseed dormant winter lawns of warm-season grasses. Withstands heavy foot traffic. Drought tolerant. Good choice for compacted soils due to deep root system that loosens soil. Plant by seed or sod in fall or spring. Recommend 7 lbs./1,000 sq. ft. Germinates in 3–7 days. Mow 1 1/2–2 in. high.

### Improved Perennial Ryegrass
*Lolium* species

Improved varieties of perennial ryegrass are longer-lived and have a greater heat tolerance than common perennial ryegrass. They have a darker green color, finer texture and blend well with other grasses in mixtures. They are drought and insect resistant. Most are easier to mow, and some varieties are cold resistant. Plant by seed or lay sod in fall or spring. Recommend 7 lbs./1,000 sq. ft. Germinates in 3–7 days. Mow 1 1/2–2 in. high.

# Cool-Season Grasses II

### Chewings Fescue
*Festuca rubra commutata*
Chewings fescue withstands dryness well and tolerates less fertile soil than the bluegrasses. A fast-growing, fine-bladed grass with medium dark green leaves, susceptible to foot traffic as it does not spread by creeping. Grows well in light shade and survives with little water. Needs frequent mowing. Susceptible to fungal diseases. Plant by seed in fall or spring. Recommend 5 lbs./1,000 sq. ft. Germinates in 8–14 days. Mow 1–2 1/2 in. high.

### Creeping Red Fescue
*Festuca rubra rubra*
The best cool-season grass for dry, shaded areas, but fares poorly in hot, wet climates. Mixes well with bluegrasses, forming a fine-textured, sturdy lawn. Medium to dark green grass that has a creeping habit. Most varieties are fast growing. Tolerates acid soil, but not low temperatures. Drought tolerant. Very susceptible to diseases in hot, wet areas. Plant by seed in fall or spring. Recommend 5 lbs./1,000 sq. ft. Germinates in 8–14 days. Mow 1/2–2 1/2 in. high.

### Hard Fescue
*Festuca ovina* var. *duriuscula*
Although not as aggressive and quick to establish as creeping and chewings fescue, hard fescue performs better in hot weather, wears better and is more disease resistant. Grows well in shade and requires little water. Leaves are coarse textured, blue-green and grow in tufts. Plant by seed in fall or spring. Recommend 5 lbs./1,000 sq. ft. Germinates in 8–14 days. Mow 1 1/2–2 1/2 in. high.

### Tall Fescue
*Festuca eliator*
Common tall fescue varieties such as Kentucky 31 have been popular low-maintenance lawn grasses in the Midsouth or transition zone of the U.S. They are heat tolerant and grow best in areas with mild winters and warm summers. The blades of common tall fescue are broad and coarse. Over the last 15 years, turfgrass researchers have developed improved varieties of turf-type tall fescue which are quickly replacing the common varieties. Plant by seed or lay sod in fall or spring. Recommend 10 lbs./1,000 sq. ft. Germinates in 7–10 days.

### Turf-Type Tall Fescue
*Festuca* species
A long-lasting grass which stands up to extreme summer heat and winter cold. Good drought tolerance with improved disease resistance. Some varieties are shade tolerant as well. Medium to dark green leaves of medium leaf texture. Plant by seed or lay sod in fall or spring. Recommend 10 lbs./1,000 sq. ft. Germinates in 7–10 days. Mow 1 1/2 in. high.

### Improved Turf-Type Tall Fescue
*Festuca* species
New varieties of tall fescue have been bred for improved finer texture, color, disease resistance, drought tolerance and shorter growth habit. These new varieties are perfect for low-maintenance showcase lawns in full sun to partial shade in hot, humid or arid climates. Improved varieties will also survive colder winters than common varieties. Plant by seed or lay sod in fall or spring. Recommend 10 lbs./1,000 sq. ft. Germinates in 7–10 days. Mow 1 1/2–2 in. high.

# Warm-Season Grasses I

### Annual Ryegrass
*Lolium multiflorum*
Quick to generate, fast growing and quick to establish, but lasting only one season. Commonly used for winter overseeding dormant warm-season grasses. Annual ryegrass flourishes during the cool months and begins to die out when permanent warm-season grasses break dormancy in the spring. Often used as a nurse grass in seed mixtures. Plant by seed in fall or spring. Recommend 7 lbs./1,000 sq. ft. Germinates in 3–7 days. Mow 1 1/2–2 in. high.

### Bahiagrass
*Paspalum notatum*
A low-maintenance grass with a very coarse texture and a wide blade. Spreads by short stolons and has an extensive root system that makes it valued for erosion control. Well adapted to coastal areas with sandy soils. Performs well in average soil in sun or part shade and heavy traffic. Fast growing, requiring frequent mowing; susceptible to fungal disease. Plant by seed or lay sod in the spring. Recommend 8 lbs./1,000 sq. ft. Germinates in 21–28 days. Mow 2–3 in. high.

### Common Bermudagrass
*Cynodon dactylon*
Very tough, medium-maintenance, heat-tolerant grass. Will tolerate minimum care but much more attractive if watered regularly. Coarse texture, low-growing, vigorous and dense. Spreads by rhizomes and stolons. Likes full sun and prefers moist soil. Goes dormant and turns brown with temperatures below 50 degrees. Improved varieties are preferred. Plant by seed in the spring. Recommend 2–3 lbs/1,000 sq. ft. Germinates in 10–20 days. Mow 3/4–1 1/2 in. high.

### Hybrid Improved Bermudagrass
*Cynodon* species
Improved varieties are more drought tolerant, finer textured and a deeper green than common Bermudagrass. Requires less water and is more disease tolerant. Often needs more frequent mowings. High fertilizer needs. Durable, but requires full sun and regular thatch control. Lay sod or plant sprigs in spring. Mow 1/2–1 in. high, using reel mower—grass will turn yellow if allowed to grow taller.

### Centipedegrass
*Eremochloa ophiuroides*
An excellent choice for poor soil and a good, low-maintenance, general-purpose lawn. Medium-textured, light green grass. Requires frequent watering. Grows well in acidic soils and resists disease and pests, even chinch bugs. A good alternative to St. Augustine grass. Highly sensitive to cold temperatures. Shallow-rooted, making it less than ideal for a play lawn. Plant by seed in spring. Recommend 1/4–1/2 lb./1,000 sq. ft. Germinates in 14–20 days.

### St. Augustine grass
*Stenotaphrum secundatum*
A very aggressive grass that is excellent for crowding out weeds. Very tough and dense; an excellent choice for recreation. Low-growing and coarse with dark green to blue-green broad blades. Grows well in both sunny and densely shaded areas. Heat tolerant. Few diseases but sensitive to chinch bugs. Requires frequent watering and thatch removal. Well suited to coastal, salty areas. Good grass for transitional areas. Lay sod or plant sprigs or plugs. Mow 1 1/2–2 in. high.

# WARM-SEASON GRASSES II

### Zoysiagrass
*Zoysia* species
One of the best grasses for heat and drought tolerance. Spreads by thick rhizomes and stolons that develop into a lush, dense, high-quality lawn. A dark green, fine-textured blade. Grows slowly, but once established makes a beautiful lawn. Warm-season and transitional zone grass that is exceptionally resistant to weeds. Resists most insects except billbugs. Grows in light shade, but goes dormant below 50 degrees. Often difficult to overseed due to density. Lay sod or plant sprigs or plugs. Mow 1–2 in. high.

### Improved Zoysiagrass
*Zoysia* species
Zoysiagrass is such a tough all-around grass for warm season and transition zone areas, it is hard to imagine it could be improved upon. One of the disadvantages of common zoysia is that it can take up to 2 years to become established. New improved varieties have reduced that time. Lay sod or plant sprigs or plugs. Mow 1–2 in. high.

### Seashore Paspalum
*Paspalum vaginatum*
Grown almost exclusively in southern California, this Australian import is an alternative to Bermudagrass. Thrives in cool, coastal regions. Aggressive and durable. Tolerant of drought, heat, pests and salty soils. Goes dormant and browns quickly in cold weather. Requires slightly more water than Bermudagrass. Likes full sun. Lay sod in spring. Mow 3/4–1 in. high.

### Saltgrass, Fults
*Pulccinellia distans*
A low-growing bunch grass that can reach a height of 16 in., but usually is mowed to medium-fine turf. Dark green leaves with excellent tolerance to salt or alkaline soils. Needs full sun. Lay sod or plant seed. Recommend 2–3 lbs./1,000 sq. ft. Germinates in 14–21 days. Mow 2 in. high.

### Dichondra
*Dichondra micrantha*
Not a grass but a bright green, glossy groundcover that wears like grass and can even be mowed. Produces a thick carpet of heart-shaped leaves that give the appearance of lush lawn. Heat tolerant and surprisingly durable. Requires frequent, thorough watering. Susceptible to pests. Weeds may be difficult to control. Plant in the spring or fall by seed, sod or plugs. Recommend 1/4–1/2 lb./1,000 sq. ft. Germinates in 14–24 days. Mow 3/4–2 in. high.

### Buffalograss
*Buchloe dactyloides*
At one time the most dominant grass across the prairies and an excellent drought- and cold-tolerant grass. Fine-textured and low-growing, buffalograss forms a dense, pale green lawn. Germinates quickly and withstands heavy foot traffic. A good low-maintenance lawn grass. Plant by seed. Recommend 1/2–1 1/2 lbs./1,000 sq. ft. Germinates in 14–20 days. Mow 1 1/2–2 in. high.

# TOOLS AND EQUIPMENT

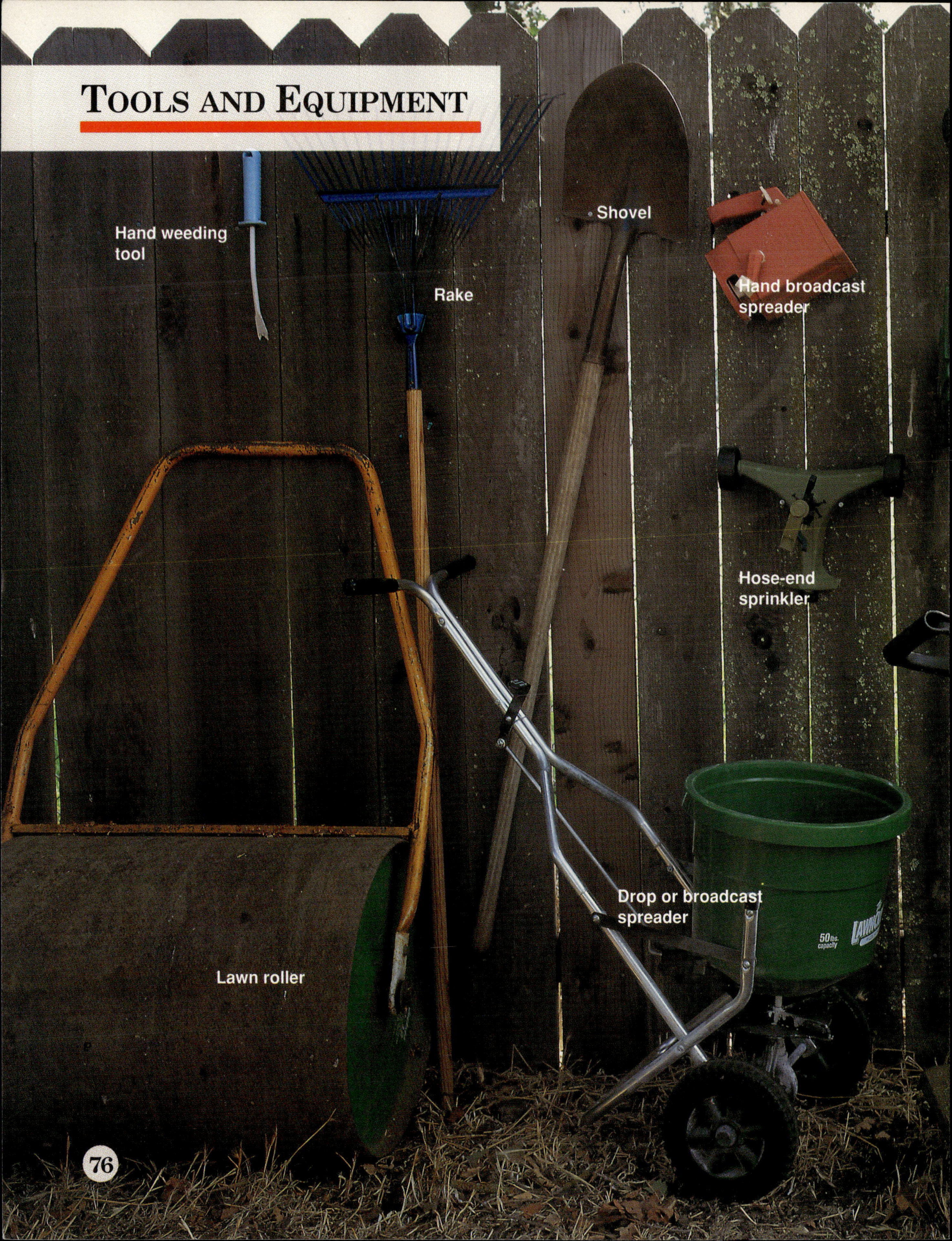

Hand weeding tool

Rake

Shovel

Hand broadcast spreader

Hose-end sprinkler

Lawn roller

Drop or broadcast spreader

76

## TOOL MAINTENANCE

Your lawn mower is the most important piece of lawn maintenance equipment. Follow the manufacturer's manual for correct care of the machine. Be sure motor oil remains at the correct level and all fitting and gaskets are kept tight to prevent oil or gas from spilling onto the lawn. Keep your mower clean. After every use, clean out grass clippings and wipe blades with an oily rag.

Always keep blades sharp. If your mower is leaving ragged, brown edges on the grass, the blade probably needs sharpening. You can sharpen the blades yourself, but you risk getting them out of balance, which will cause the mower to vibrate. Have a professional do the job; it is not expensive. Consult your owner's manual to find out how to remove and reinstall the blades safely so you won't have to take the mower to the shop.

Store the mower in a dry place. Drain the fuel tank for winter storage and in the spring, change the oil, clean the spark plugs and refill the gas tank.

Also maintain your other lawn care equipment. Spreaders for fertilizer, lime or sulfur should always be emptied, washed and thoroughly dried after use. Many fertilizers will cause the metal parts to corrode.

Irrigation systems will need to be flushed and drained in cool weather areas to prevent freezing. All portable hoses should be drained and stored for the winter.

Large equipment, like dethatching machines and aerating machines, are costly and best rented as needed. Unless you do a lot of gardening, rotary tillers are also best rented.

# INDEX

**A**
Acidity, soil, 24, 31
Aerification
  steps, 14-15
  timing for, 66-67
Agricultural Extension Service, 24
*Agropyron repens*, 57
*Agrostis stolonifera pulustris*, 68
Alkaline, soil, 24, 31
Amendments
  planting, 47
  soil, 28-29
  timing for, 66
Annual ryegrass (*Lolium multiflorum*), 72
Anti-siphon valves, 33
Automatically-controlled time clock, 34

**B**
Bahiagrass (*Paspalum notatum*), 72
Bare spots
  due to, 8
  repairing, 12
Bentgrass, 14
Bermudagrass, 14, 36, 39, 66, 72
Black plastic, 18-19
Blending varieties, 41
Blue Fescue (*Festuca ovina glauca*), 60
Bluegrass lawns
  fusarium blight in, 13
  shade and, 37
Broadcast fertilizer spreading, 55
Broadleafed weeds, 56
Brown patch disease, 12
*Buchloe dactyloides*, 75
Buffalograss (*Buchloe dactyloides*), 66, 75

**C**
Centipedegrass (*Eremochloa ophiuroides*), 39, 73
Chemicals
  removing lawn with, 18
  *see also* Fertilizers
Chewings fescue (*Festuca rubra communtata*), 70
Clay soil, 25
Climate, 7, 36, 43, 64
Climate zone map, 36, 64
Common bermudagrass (*Cynodon dactylon*), 72
Common Kentucky bluegrass (*Poa pratensis*), 68
Compost, 49
Conditioners, soil, 28
Control valve, 33
Cool-season grasses
  bentgrass, 14
  climate for, 64, 67
  Kentucky bluegrass, 14
  planting, 39, 45-46
  types listed, 68-71
Crabgrass (*Digitaria sanguinalis*), 56
Creeping bentgrass (*Agrostis stolonifera pulustris*), 68
Creeping red fescue (*Festuca rubra rubra*), 70
Crop seeds, 42
*Cynodon dactylon*, 72
*Cynodon* species, 72

**D**
Damaged areas, 12
Dandelion (*Taraxacum officinale*), 56
Dethatching
  as maintenance, 59
  steps, 14-15
  timing for, 66-67
Dichondra (*Dichondra micrantha*), 60, 75
*Dichondra micrantha*, 60, 75
*Digitaria sanguinalis*, 56
Diseases
  characterized by, 9, 13
  maintenance controlling, 56-57
Drainage, 22-23
Drop spreading fertilizer, 55
Drought
  groundcovers and, 62
  lawns and resistance to, 36, 51
  regional differences, 66
Dry fertilizers, 54

**E**
English Ivy (*Hedera* species), 61
Equipment
  drop spreader, 76
  hand broadcast spreader, 77
  hand edger, 77
  hand weeding tool, 76
  hoe, 77
  hose-end sprinkler, 76
  lawn roller, 77
  maintenance of, 77
  mower, 52-53, 77
  professional, 10
  rake, 76
  rotary tiller, 18-19, 26-27, 48
  seed/fertilizer spreader, 44
  shovel, 77
  sod cutter, 18
  soil sampling tube, 24
  soil test kits, 24
  string trimmer, 77
  trenching machine, 32
  water hose, 77
  water roller, 47
*Eremochloa ophiuroides*, 73
*Euonymus fortunei*, 61
*Euphorbia maculata*, 56

**F**
Fertilizers
  applying, 54-55
  choosing, 54
  dry and liquid, 54
  during planting, 47
  nutrient measurements, 54
  organic and inorganic, 54
  regional differences in, 66
  repairing burns, 12
  timing for, 7, 57
  watering, 55
Fescues
  advantages of, 36-37
  types of, 40, 42, 60, 70-71
*Festuca eliator*, 71
*Festuca ovina* var. *duriuscula*, 70
*Festuca ovina glauca*, 60
*Festuca rubra communtata*, 70
*Festuca rubra rubra*, 70
*Festuca* species, 71
Foot traffic, 13, 59
'Fults' *Pulccinellia distans*, 13
Fungus, 13
Fusarium blight, 13

**G**
Gallons per minute (GPM), 32, 34
Grading
  lawns and, 22-23, 44
  watering and, 51
Grass weeds, 56-57
Groundcovers
  easy care of, 60
  planting, 62
  types of, 60-61
Grubs, 9, 13

**H**
Hard fescue (*Festuca ovina* var. *duriuscula*), 70
*Hedera* species, 61
Hybrid improved Bermudagrass (*Cynodon* species), 72

**I**
Improved Kentucky bluegrass (*Poa* species), 69
Improved perennial ryegrass (*Lolium* species), 69
Improved zoysiagrass (*Zoysia* species), 74
In-ground irrigation system
  control valve and connections, 33
  installing, 34-35
  selecting materials, 32
Inorganic fertilizers, 54
Insect damage, 9
Irrigation system
  installing in-ground, 32-35
  maintenance of, 77

**K**
Kentucky bluegrass, 14, 36, 40, 41, 69

**L**
Lawn edgings, 21
Lawn grasses
  Bermudagrass varieties, 36, 39, 66
  blending varieties, 41
  bluegrass, 37
  buffalograss, 66
  centipedegrass, 39
  choosing, 6, 40, 42-43
  crop seeds, 42
  drought resistant, 36
  fertilizer requirements, 55
  fesucues, 36-37, 42
  'Fults' *Pulccinellia distans*, 13
  Kentucky bluegrass, 14, 37, 41
  mixtures, 40-41
  nurse grass, 41
  perennial ryegrass, 37, 41
  planting, 38-39
  regional differences in, 66-67
  St. Augustine grass, 14, 37, 39
  sun tolerance, 36
  wearability of, 37
  zoysiagrass varieties, 36, 39, 66
  *see also* Cool-season grasses; Warm-season grasses

78

Lawns
    alternatives to turfgrass, 60–62
    bluegrass, 13
    drought-resistant, 36
    evaluating, 9
    first mowing, 52
    getting started on new, 8
    grading and drainage, 22–23, 44
    installing edgings, 21
    minor repair, 12
    new home sites, 21
    preparing site for, 20–21
    removing old, 18–19
    shade and, 37
    steps to planting new, 6–7
    sun tolerance and, 36
    watering established, 51
    wearability of, 37
    *see also* Maintenance; Planting lawns; Renovation program
Lime, 7, 30–31, 57
Liquid fertilizers, 54
Loam soil, 25
*Lolium multiflorum*, 72
*Lolium perenne*, 69
*Lolium* species, 69

## M

Maintenance
    annual, 56
    fall care, 57
    irrigation systems, 77
    long-term, 58
    pest control by, 13
    3–5 year plan, 59
    tool and equipment, 77
    weed and pest control, 56–57
Manifold, 33
Mixtures (grass), 41
Mower, 52–53, 76–77
Mowing
    first, 52
    good practices, 53
Mulch, 45

## N

New lawns, 6–7
    *see also* Lawns
Nurse grass, 41
Nutrients
    soil testing for, 24
    testing for soil, 7

## O

Organic fertilizers, 54
Organic materials
    adding, 28–29
    adding during planting, 48–49
Overseeding
    benefits of, 16
    regional differences in, 66
    tips, 17, 57
    winter, 16
*Oxalis corniculata*, 57
Oxalis (*Oxalis corniculata*), 57

## P

Pachysandra (*Pachysandra terminalis*), 61
*Pachysandra terminalis*, 61
*Paspalum notatum*, 72
*Paspalum vaginatum*, 74
Pavement salt, 13
Perennial ryegrass, 37, 40, 41, 43
Perennial ryegrass (*Lolium perenne*), 69
Periwinkle (*Vinca minor*), 61
Pests, 56
PH
    adjusting, 7, 31, 66
    brown patch disease and, 12
    soil testing for, 24
*Plantago* species, 57
Plantain (*Plantago* species), 57
Planting lawns
    from seed, 7, 38, 44–45
    from sod, 7, 38, 46–47
    from sprigs and plugs, 7, 39, 48–49
    timing for, 57
    watering and, 45, 49–51
Plugging
    planting by, 7, 39
    watering, 51
*Poa pratensis*, 68
*Poa* species, 69
*Poa trivialis*, 68
Pressure per square inch (PSI), 34
Professional help, 10–11
*Pulcinellia distans*, 13, 75
PVC pipe, 32

## Q

Quackgrass (*Agropyron repens*), 57

## R

Rainfall, 67
Raking leaves, 57
Reel mowers, 53
Renovation program
    assessing, 9, 13
    dethatching and aerification, 14–15
    overseeding, 16–17
    *see also* Lawns
Rotary mowers, 53
Rotary tiller
    maintenance of, 77
    using a, 18–19, 26–27, 48
Rough-stalk bluegrass (*Poa trivialis*), 68
"Runners," 49
Ryegrass, 37, 40, 41, 43, 69

## S

Saltgrass, Fults (*Pulcinellia distans*), 75
Sand, adding to soil, 28–29
Sandy soil, 25
Seashore paspalum (*Paspalum vaginatum*), 74
Seeds
    choosing grass, 6, 40, 42–43
    germination, 45
    planting by, 7, 38, 44–45
    watering, 50
Self-draining valve, 32
Shade
    grass selection and, 37
    growth and, 9
Shutoff gate valve, 33
Silt soil, 25
Sod cutter, 18
Sodding
    planting by, 7, 38
    watering after, 50
Soil
    acidity and alkalinity, 24, 31
    adding lime or sulfur, 30–31
    amending, 28–29
    clay, 25
    compaction, 13–14, 59
    determining type of, 7
    loam, 25
    preparation, 6, 21, 26–27, 44
    preparation for groundcovers, 62
    probes to measure watering, 51
    sandy, 25
    silt, 25
    testing, 7, 24
    thin growth and, 9
Soil test kits, 24
Spotted spurge (*Euphorbia maculata*), 56
Sprigs
    planting, 7, 39, 48–49
    watering, 51
Sprinklers, 32
*Stenotaphrum secundatum*, 73
Stolons, *see* Sprigs
St. Augustine grass (*Stenotaphrum secundatum*), 14, 37, 39, 73
Sulfur, 7, 30–31
Sun, exposure to, 36

## T

Tall fescue (*Festuca eliator*), 71
*Taraxacum officinale*, 56
Thatch, 14
Tiller, *see* Rotary tiller
Tools, *see* Equipment
Topsoil, 23
Trees, 23
Trenching machine, 32
Turf-type tall fescue (*Festuca* species), 71

## V

*Vinca minor*, 61

## W

Warm-season grasses
    climate for, 64, 66
    growth of, 39
    planting, 45–46
    types listed, 72–75
Watering
    after fertilizing, 55
    germination and, 45
    groundcovers, 62
    planting methods and, 49–51
    regional differences in, 66
    soil compaction and, 59
Water roller, 47
Wearability, lawn, 37
Weeds
    defining, 8
    in groundcovers, 62
    maintenance control of, 56–57
    repairing spots, 12
    types listed, 56
Winter creeper (*Euonymus fortunei*), 61

## Z

Zone, *see* Climate zone map
Zoysiagrass (*Zoysia* species), 36, 39, 66, 74
*Zoysia* species, 74

## A Note From NK Lawn and Garden Co.

For more than 100 years, since its founding in Minneapolis, Minnesota, NK Lawn and Garden has provided gardeners with the finest quality seed and other garden products.

We doubt that our leaders, Jesse E. Northrup and Preston King, would recognize their seed company today, but gardeners everywhere in the U.S. still rely on NK Lawn and Garden's knowledge and experience at planting time.

We are pleased to be able to share this practical experience with you through this ongoing series of easy-to-use gardening books.

Here you'll find hundreds of years of gardening experience distilled into easy-to-understand text and step-by-step pictures. Every popular gardening subject is included.

As you use the information in these books, we hope you'll also try our lawn and garden products. They're available at your local garden retailer.

There's nothing more satisfying than a successful, beautiful garden. There's something special about the color of blooming flowers and the flavor of home-grown garden vegetables.

We understand how special you feel about growing things—and NK Lawn and Garden feels the same way, too. After all, we've been a friend to gardeners everywhere since 1884.